Trilogy
of thoughts from a
GRUMPY
innovator

This is the first edition, September 2020

Twitter: @grumpyinnovator
Email: costas@grumpyinnovator.com
Web: grumpyinnovator.com

ISBN 979-868-393-9465

Kudos

"9/10 ... it also turns out his book is touched with genius ... aphorisms, many of which are as pointed as they are funny. If only all business books could be this entertaining."
Tim Hulse
Editor @ British Airways, Business Book of the Month

★ ★ ★ ★ - "This book is a *lot* of fun."
BookIdeas.*com*

"Flippantly Flipping Fabulous. An antidote of sunshine for true innovators and intrapreneurs struggling in the web of corporate ambiguity!"
Arun Prabhu,
Commercial Innovation Director @ Arla Foods

★ ★ ★ ★ - "A collection of thoughts and observations regarding the bizarre and illogical world of commercial innovation"
San Francisco Book Review

"I was grumpy wishing I had written it. It now sits officially on the top of the 'books I will steal from shamelessly' pile."
Dave McCaughan,
Director of Strategic Planning @ McCann

"This book is packed with witty observations that make serious points"
Frank Dillon
Business Editor @ The Irish Times

thoughts from a
GRUMPY
innovator

written & illustrated by costas papaikonomou

This is the second edition, June 2013

Twitter:	@grumpyinnovator
Email:	costas@grumpyinnovator.com
Web:	grumpyinnovator.com

to Patricia, Spiro and Dimi

who melt my grumpiness away, instantly.

[
If the grass weren't greener on the other side, humanity would still be in caves with no intention to mow any of it.
]

Thoughts from a Grumpy Innovator

This little book is the narcissistic result of posting thoughts onto Twitter™ over a number of years, mostly on the topic of mass market innovation.

A couple of themes have emerged, which form the chapters of this book – each with a central narrative, thought or plain grump.

My interest is in the intrinsic, systemic reasons commercial innovation works the way it does. Which I can summarize for you right here as being quite *odd*, to say the least.

If you're looking for a business management book with clear-cut tips and tricks, then I'm sorry. You won't find an extensive list of innovation success stories to copy, nor an Innovate-O-Matic toolbox to plunder. There is no 12-step process that will guarantee a successful launch of your new idea.

So I'm afraid I can't promise you'll make millions after reading this book, but I do hope you'll smile every now and then.

Premise:
I'm grumpy and I shouldn't be

Anyone celebrating the tenacity of successful innovators is probably ignoring the far larger number of tenacious idiots pursuing bad ideas. If you think about the classic description of what character traits help people succeed in turning an innovative idea into a profitable business stream – winners and losers at this particular game are frighteningly similar:

- *Dogged determination*
- *Blind devotion to their idea*
- *Unshakable confidence, against all odds*

There must be a fine line between getting it very right or very wrong. In fact, I think there's a paradox hidden in there.

Companies are structured entities, with defined procedures and efficient processes that ensure things get done. Even the messiest of businesses are organized to some level. In stark contrast, the *reality* they operate in is unpredictable, fluid, ugly and most of all: immense. In this simple contrast lies a beautiful paradox: it is the reason there will always be new opportunities & needs for new things *and* it is the main reason for failing at successfully doing so. The attributes that guarantee new opportunities are the opposite of what an efficient corporate system thrives upon.

The chart below shows how the four capabilities crucial to running a business are hampered in the context of innovation[1]. Within the neatly controlled corporate

---

[1] *Yes, you can slice business up many other ways too. But this particular way happens to work well for my story.*

ecosystem, they do as they're asked to and all is fine – as long as they keep looking inward.

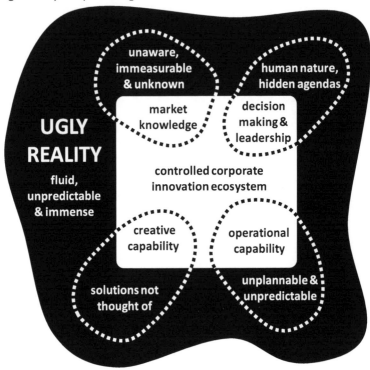

I've found most of the failures in innovation can be brought back to individuals and teams in denial of the reality outside of their campus walls, totally unnecessarily.

This little book holds some of the thoughts I had seeing this happen. If you have experience in the innovation arena, you may recognize attitudes, situations and odd behaviours. Don't worry, we'll keep those our little secret.

Costas Papaikonomou
The Hague, May 2012

The Art Of Beanbags & Funny Hats

**I KNOW IT'S JUST A BOX.
BUT WAIT 'TILL YOU HEAR THE SINGLE-
MINDED BENEFIT.**

The Art Of Beanbags & Funny Hats

Every solution has a problematic history, by definition. In that sense, the skills behind successful innovation could be framed as the ability to create solutions for problems before anyone realizes what a nuisance they are. Successful innovation is not about dreaming up what would be science fiction today, but about foreseeing what will be plain vanilla tomorrow.

You can imagine most creative professionals do not find that thought particularly motivating, which is why such a large chunk of this discipline appears to be about putting the 'art' of being creative up on an ever higher pedestal than the output it generates. Much of the world of innovation is populated by creative gurus, visionary high priests who scatter riddles across 2x2 diagrams to paint your future portfolio. Well, implement creativity like a religion and you'll need miracles to be successful.

Breakthrough ideas often feed creative egos, not consumer needs. If anything, successful new products and services are like the weather; about 90% the same as yesterday's products. This isn't to say the world needs no game changing innovation; it's merely that too many businesses waste time looking *outside* the box when their market still has plenty room left to grow and differentiate *inside* it.

For some of the world's leading companies and brand teams, success seems based on historical serendipities, luck, or lack of competition. Nevertheless stupendous amounts of money are wasted on turning an innovation project into a show.

Maybe creative capability is genuinely seen as something much more difficult than it really is? Then again, if Edison really meant it being 1% inspiration and 99% perspiration he would have invented deodorant. Or GoreTex. What's making this all so difficult?

- *A **belief you need to be uncomfortable to work outside your comfort zone**. Funny hats, beanbags and humiliating 'energizers'. A whole industry has grown around the mantra that in order for people to take creative risk, they should be made to feel even more uneasy than they already are.*

- ***Features rather than benefits?** The first decade of the new millennium brought high-end software and technology into consumers' daily lives, in a way previously unheard of. With it came an insatiable drive for new features in order to provide marginal difference between devices and social media, a trend which seems to be trickling down into physical mass markets. What happened to thinking about benefits first? If anything, added features often introduce another hurdle between a consumer and the benefit they're trying to get from a product. They also distract attention from the core that's attracting consumers to your products.*

- ***Re-inventing predecessors' wheels.** In many corporate ecosystems the responsibility for innovation lies with the marketing department, a discipline known for high job rotation. Which from an innovation standpoint is fine, as long as the track record is kept diligently. And often it isn't. New marketing & brand managers waste plenty of their time redeveloping ideas that have bombed many times before.*

- ***Believing your own spin.** In mature FMCG categories, the reality is that everyone needs to push the envelope on what can be claimed in order to stand out from the* *crowd. But the line between substantiated claims and spin is thin. No problem. Think homeopathy. In practice this leads to claims that sound credible in respect of the brand equity or previous claims, rather than being based on new developments. And that's when a credible myth all too easily becomes the new benchmark for truth.*

- **Marketing executive's lives and their consumers' lives couldn't be further apart.** *Having empathy with your target consumer does not mean bringing to market only the products you'd buy yourself. On the contrary. Corporate professionals dealing with mass market innovation tend to belong to a society's top 2% income level, with the other 98% being their target. This target is seldom as interested in 'on-the-go' or 'stress relief' or 'personalization' as one may hope.*

So what to do? Well, first of all assume there is a solution for any creative problem and trust that it won't require black magic to uncover it.

- **Make time, not space.** *You don't need to be in a Hungarian lakeside castle to be creative. In fact, the environment is mostly irrelevant as long as it's comfortable – that's why beds and bathtubs ignite new ideas. What you need most is TIME. Uninterrupted time to work on the innovation task, alone or as a group – to understand the problem, the context and to work on solutions. If you do your homework, a couple of days is often enough to crack even the toughest nuts.*

- **An un-filtered look at the (consumer) context.** *All you need is some rigor in pinpointing what the real needs are, for relevant answers to pop out painlessly. Real insight carries far. Note this involves more listening and reading to what consumers actually say and less reading of macro-economic trends or your brand vision deck.*

- *Cherish the small incremental ideas.* Most growth challenges do not require breakthrough solutions. Give small ideas a chance.

- *Reality first – then brand equity.* Stay in touch with the physical attributes of your product before getting carried away by what you wish were possible. The touch, the smell, the chemistry, the taste, the sounds... Nothing beats a trip to your factory and R&D lab before getting to work on a consumer problem.

Maybe all this is best summarized as follows:

Keep these ...

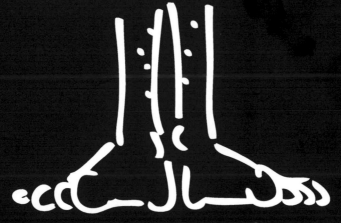

... on the ground.

Wishful thinking and blue-sky ideation are absolutely fine, but they are a transfer station, not the end destination of your effort. Even the wildest ideas must come back to earth in order to become part of an operational process that can make a business thrive.

"I just found out someone else had exactly the same idea before me" - poor sod uncovering the truth about all ideas.

Great innovations versus duds... One is full of flaws, a budget vampire, ruins careers, virtually no chance of success. The other is a dud.

Our best flashes of inspiration happen when having shower, which is really practical with the 99% perspiration then kicking in.

Solutions without problems are even worse time vampires than problems without solutions.

Just like you shouldn't shop for food on an empty stomach, you shouldn't innovate on an empty development funnel. Anything would then be good enough.

"The heart of a lion and the mind of a dandelion" – great recipe for creative success.

Good ideas and bad ideas have one thing in common: at first glance, both often look like bad ideas. Or was it the other way around?

Ask not how to make the future more futuristic, ask instead how to make the past more old-fashioned.

Planning to have an idea while sitting at your desk is no different from answering emails while having a shower.

If you're wondering whether that idea is good enough, it probably isn't. If only because your insecurity would stand in the way of bringing even the best idea to market.

Industries succeeding through in-the-box thinking: pizza delivery, caskets, multiple choice input devices and flight data recording.

An un-creative person in a beanbag with a funny hat & a Hawaiian shirt on is still un-creative. But now armed with false confidence.

Don't reinvent a wheel that merely needs reframing.

Step 1 to finding a solution is realising there is one. Step 0 is admitting you haven't got one.

If you find yourself needing the word "because" more than once when introducing a new idea to an audience, either the idea or the audience need sharpening.

The good thing that success and failure have in common is that they both break the status quo.

Your Blue Sky innovation may have patches of rain.

There are no bad ideas, only unappreciative audiences.

Like with children, you sometimes need to discipline your ideas to ensure they grow into mature beings.

Enlightenment comes from small, sweet observations, yoga, Buddha and lamp posts.

Good ideas tend to take more time to develop than bad ones. Sadly, spending forever developing an idea doesn't guarantee it'll be good.

Only in innovation can evolution and creationism comfortably coexist.

Slapping 'New Formula' or 'Improved Recipe' onto an existing product's label is the innovator's equivalent of writer's block.

When encountering a road block on an innovation roadmap, finding the solution will also transform the path itself and lead to a new destination.

There are those who see their bodies as convenient carriers to move their brain around; and those who just see their bodies.

There is a fine line beyond which asking lots of questions shifts from being a token of curiosity to one of paralyzing insecurity.

The story of this particular innovation project I'm in would make a fantastic musical.

Like real children, ideas need most attention when they're tired and start annoying everyone.

If your new ideas aren't impressing the old folks, share some of your old ideas with the new folks.

**WE CREATED THIS COLLAGE TO
EXPRESS CONSUMERS' EMOTIONAL
EXPERIENCE OF "1KG"**

Don't expect a serendipitous solution when, you're concentrating really hard to find one.

Jobs where creativity is frowned upon: airline pilot, doctors, taxi driver, accountant, judge, taxman, garbage collector, son-in-law.

If at first you succeed, try, try again anyway.

The bottom line is that 'systematized creativity' is like 'creative accounting': it's a bit naughty and everyone secretly wants some.

Prehistoric Man learned how to catch fish. Industrial Age Man learned how to catch and sell lotsa fish. Z-Gen Man learned to tweet #Where2BuyShushi.

Big ideas have only small audiences, initially.

Great ideas usually come in pairs. First a fabulous one, then an even more fabulous one. But only if you don't lose your cool after the first one.

When you bump into a massive barrier... you have in fact found what will eventually become the way forward.

On left/right brain modes. When chatting on the phone... Should I hold my wife to my left ear and my accountant to my right?

Mediocre idea? Write it on the back of a napkin, photograph it and project it full-screen in PowerPoint. If it still fails, it IS mediocre.

Amazing how Einstein didn't need Einstein quotes for inspiration.

Beware of breakthrough concepts that are designed to feed their creators' egos instead of consumer needs. They can be deceitfully appealing.

People want holes, not drills. Sorry, I mean hooks, not holes. No, decorations on walls, not hooks. No, a nice house!

A compromise is not a solution; it's not even supposed to be. Unless you manage to turn it into a feature and call it a 'hybrid'.

Evolution: the path from A to B. Revolution: the leap from A to C. Game Changer: the path from A to sliced bread.

Things that are exceptionally fast tend to also be exceptionally fragile. And exceptionally far off mark when aimed incorrectly.

"Temporarily removes nagging sense of guilt" would work as an on-pack claim on most food products. Does anyone know if EFSA will allow this?

* SPOILER ALERT * Box-o-chocolate style concepts to personalize product experience will BOMB in concept tests, except in Chocolates category.

On the development timeline, innovation is the bit that happens in between celebrations.

As a lone brand manager, you sometimes find yourself lost, lacking ideas, vision. And THAT's when the bean bag & post-its business gets you.

It's amazing how much stuff you sometimes need to remove from a three word idea headline, in order to get through to the ten word essence.

The level of brilliance of an idea is not defined by the idea itself, but by the audience exposed to it. So choose your audience wisely. I mean dumbly.

When wondering what benefits to add to your proposition, don't forget to remove a few too.

The perfect packaging is one that's made itself obsolete. Yet the ambition to develop 'nothing' is a leap too far for most pack developers.

All the lateral, right brain thinking I've been doing has made my left brain feel constrained & stifled. Time for out-of-the-box reasoning.

I wonder if the length of an innovation pipeline correlates with the attention span of the people responsible for filling it?

If you're allowed to bring just one thing to creative problem solving workshop; bring an answer.

OK, time for some of my own medicine. From now on, I pledge to have 10% better ideas.

Great, so we selected the sensible, safe idea from that batch of wacky concepts. Now let's build some fun into it, because it's a bit bland. #NeverGonnaHappen

Fact: workshop warm-up with armpit farts and alphabet burping does not raise a group's collaborative creativity, but man is it funny.

Well, as a last resort when looking for new USP's, you could choose to use your own product for a while & find out first hand.

Does your new idea look equally attractive with helmet hair and without make-up? Then don't hold back and embrace the future.

Test your true love of an idea by considering having it tattooed.

Make sure to have plenty of sex before an ideation workshop because even if you then have no ideas, you'll still have had plenty of sex.

Bad ideas can be cunningly disguised as good ones. Be prepared and arm yourself with the infallible power of hindsight.

LSD is pretty bad at creativity, unless you give a human as a tool.

Try explaining the value of a single-minded concept benefit to schizophrenic marketing manager.

Relying on your 1st idea as your best idea is like expecting the idea of the century to come in the 1st decade.

No two snowflakes are alike. Ditto for cornflakes and skin flakes or any other flake you may meet today.

If you look hard and concentrate enough, you'll miss the solutions right under your nose.

If your product name sounds like something from a 50's monster movie, a 60's SF movie, or a 70's exploitation movie... Reconsider.

Use it or lose it: a truth for your creative mind, your best people, your muscle mass, your front row seat and your car keys.

The success of an idea depends on the audience, the timing and the capability to manage cash flow. Much less the idea itself.

Creative Problem Solving is the intriguing arena where complex technical problems can be resolved by blistering air guitar solos.

The fact you have nothing better doesn't mean what you have is good enough. Which is of course what originally drove us to walking upright.

Don't clutter a great idea with too much "Reason To Believe". You'll look like you're trying to cover up something, like the crooks in those old Columbo episodes.

When was the last time you surprised someone with a present they asked for? Co-creation works by uncovering needs, not by asking for ideas.

Funny hats and beanbags in innovation sessions will help you creatively mess up your hair and wrinkle your trousers.

Probably the single most important factor in progressing difficult innovation initiatives is getting enough sleep, for all involved.

85% of inventors are too optimistic about the chances of success for their big idea. 10% are realistic. The successful 5% are very lucky.

Knowledge and innovation are fuelled by curiosity, so their greatest inhibitor is not ignorance but apathy. Or worse, bigotry. "

It was a dark and stormy night..." - Marketing manager about to write a massively verbose consumer insight statement.

"Well, 2x2's are so old hat of course. Experience the raw power of our new 3x3" - boardroom consultant up-selling.

Newton explained that a system in balance won't accelerate nor decelerate. Go figure, work-life balance coaches.

I suspect most people complaining about lack of good ideas simply don't know what a good idea looks like.

Yo Momma innovate so bad she lined up at the dole office to collect her concept's benefits.

Perfectionists and slackers have in common that neither knows when something is good enough.

Whoever talks about creative thought being as liberating as flying is deliberately excluding the analogy of endless runway taxiing.

Be aware that the big idea that will make you millions may currently be disguised as the rattling prototype that doesn't really work. Yet.

Get your final copy written by a native speaker; but not before the underlying proposition is done by a foreigner with half the vocabulary.

MOM, DAD – HE'S A CREATIVE.

If you can't explain your proposition with only hand gestures and maybe a crayon, make it simpler. Practice in a foreign language.

> **Inside every grey office mouse sits a vibrant creative soul, screaming to please be left inside where it's nice and quiet.**

Hinged cell phones went extinct because of the discomfort for men with sideburns.

I'm writing this Organic Fair Trade food concept and need your help. Is "moral superiority" an emotional or rational consumer benefit?

In concept development, one word often says more than a thousand pictures.

Innovation success is as much defined by bravery as it is by the quality of the idea. Having opposable thumbs helps too.

Of course, for dreams to be broken, they require some structural integrity first.

No, you can't go out and look for something random. It wouldn't be random, would it?

"Let's revitalize this category with a new product everyone will love" – team embarking on product development which everyone will hate.

"Now watch me chart your future portfolio by using this amazing 2x2 matrix" - opening sentence to pseudo-scientific marketing extravaganza.

Innovation success factors: total dedication, long hours, your last money – they'll guarantee it wasn't lack of effort that thwarted your Big Idea.

Ideagnosia - the inability to recognize a good idea right in front of you.

You can't cancel out bad ideas by adding good ones. That just doubles your workload.

Speeding up an ideation workshop fearing creativity will run out is like speeding up painting a room fearing the paint will run out.

Set your objective clearly, focus, be confident, work hard and you'll be sure to miss the better opportunities that pop up on the way there.

Water and Air have remarkably low PR value as magic ingredients; even though they're two of the very few we actually can't do without.

The quality of an idea is defined by the sender, the receiver and the amount of noise on the line.

Imagine someone has to use your user-friendly feature 20 times an hour, 8 hours a day. Is it then still user-friendly or just fancy looking?

Stretching far out of the box and then raking it back in works great for innovative ideas; but very poorly for romantic relationships.

Contrary to Archimedes' findings - when you're up shit creek, hot air sinks and dense, grounded stuff flies.

Things that struggle to find new owners in the 2nd hand market: toothbrushes, 35mm cameras, underwear and creative ideas. #NotInventedHere

I've just upgraded my lucky socks to lucky pyjamas. Hope my clients don't notice.

Creative Entropy - Once you've made something simple into a complicated mess, you can never make it simple again.

No matter what your creative facilitator wants you to do, you cannot focus outside the box. #HairSplitting

Creative revenge is best served bold.

Creating ideas alone is like drinking alone. Less fun, less productive, potentially embarrassing and a sign that something else is wrong.

Bottled iceberg & glacier water? I thought we were trying to keep those frozen. Or is it sustainable by freezing some Rhine tap water back?

SCREW THE INNOVATION FUNNEL.
I WANT TO GO HOME.

It's so easy to make it all very complicated.

If your big fab idea is so radically new there's nothing to compare it to, you have a massive positioning problem coming up.

From a constructive point of view, the row of windows in an airplane is like a massive perforated tear-strip to separate top & bottom halves.

Champagne for the winning idea. Real pain for what usually happens next.

Raising the innovative capability of a nation: Ask not what your country can do for you. Ask what you can do contrary.

The innovation space for new magic ingredients in food is about the size of the logic gap that both oxygen AND anti-oxidants are perceived as beneficial.

Only when facing deadlines do you finally notice the beauty of staring out the window watching the weather pass by.

Having to invent a new word to describe your idea is sometimes good, but usually very bad.

The ability to take ownership of something you didn't ask for is a mind-set to admire.

If you want the CMO to be happy, make sure the CFO is happy first.

Before launch, do check your original insight was a real one and not some spin you made up long ago just to get the project signed off.

Even in the most powerful and diverse ideation sessions, temptation calls to simply pick the new ideas that landed inside the box.

On word-smithing concepts. Ask yourself "will this really affect the final execution in any way?". Then find something useful to do.

Hey positioning guru - what have you redone for me lately?!

Funny how before social media, companies actually had to go out and speak with their consumers.

"Ceci n'est pas une pipe-ligne d'innovation!" - Magritte being really annoying in his first job in consumer goods.

The best R&D teams are happy to make the brand teams believe it's their own great idea. We can keep a secret.

The easiest place to start improving your products is reducing or removing the trade-offs of using it. Yes, there is always a trade-off.

"Would it generate enough excitement for a crowd funded business case?" - a good way to mentally check if your idea is truly breakthrough.

Aaargh. I always forget where I parked my ideas.

It takes three to Tango, unless one of the two can play the bandoneón while dancing.

Big ideas go unnoticed, unless you sprinkle lots of small ideas around them as reference to highlight the difference.

The question isn't if there's possibly a better idea (yes there will be), the question is if it'll be yours and if it's worth waiting for.

I have a hunch that successful artists are in fact successful businesspeople with an artsy hobby to fill the gaps between deals.

Innovation oxymorons: "extensive brief", "exploratory focus group", "emergency procedure", "low-risk opportunity" and "creative process".

Hey breakthrough innovators - yes, you can bend the rules of law & regulation. You cannot bend the laws of physics.

Even with the best intent, brainstorming for problems is never helpful.

"He who looks up, sees no borders" - but does trip over the kids toys all the time.

I think I'll re-interpret Einstein's quote as "Take things as serious as possible, but not too serious".

Invite the whole team to evaluate your idea and I guarantee you'll hear reasons it won't work that you had never imagined possible.

If your design team's presentation is laid out in Comic Sans, tread carefully.

When working on breakthrough product innovation, don't forget to check if you have the brands to deliver them through.

"No - 'rewarding' and 'gratifying' are two VERY DIFFERENT emotional benefits!" - Never wordsmith concepts with a OCD marketer.

"We want something with an eye and a globe" - starting point for too many logo design briefs and end point for too many un-briefed designs.

Are you re-writing that concept to convince your consumer or your market research department?

Nice shirt! I see you fell for the "no iron" on-pack claim.

You know the R&D prototype presentation is going to be fun if the presenter puts in earplugs and steps back 6ft before pressing 'start'.

Beware of brand managers who talk eloquently and extensively about their brand, without referring to the actual products.

"This concept has enough substance to excite a homeopath"

Passion backed by numbers will always beat mere passion.

"It's SO annoying when people check emails during my presentation. Or worse, just start talking" - Stewardess after her flight safety instruction.

"Help, I'm A Celebrity Get Me Outta Here" - the attitude amongst most marketing managers working on the same brand for longer than 3 years.

Give me a reason why - and I'll give you a conflicting one.

A: "Let's do an innovation marathon!" B: "That's our normal procedure."

"I'd like to do more strategic work; but I don't really have a plan on how to do this" - the irony is lost on the thousands of creatives saying this.

"6!! I NEED A 6th... NOW!!" - Desperate marketing manager whose quadruple promise has just been trumped by the competition's 5-in-1 claim.

"We need to explain our benefit with a broad, sweeping metaphor, consumers love that" - Marketer who needs to get more specific, quickly.

The modern equivalent of the classic concept format (insight-promise-RTB-tagline) is written as WTF-LOL-OMG-Like(x).

You may need to go back through your notes a few times to find what you weren't looking for.

I'm ditching the beanbags and funny hats. I hear it's much more effective to run creative workshops while driving, showering and sleeping.

The Evil Twin
Of Operational Excellence

**THE COST-OF-GOODS OF THIS PRODUCT IS
ABSOLUTELY AWFUL. HOW ABOUT AERATING
IT AND CALLING IT A MOUSSE?**

The Evil Twin
Of Operational Excellence

Operational Excellence - the mantra that came into fashion in the early nineties of the previous century and one that is still fanatically preached across the globe. This is the world of Lean, Six Sigma, 5s, TQM.

It assumes businesses thrive by being operationally perfect.

Paradoxically, many of the process superstars that grew to dominate their markets through Operational Excellence have fallen prey to its stillborn twin: *Systemic Inertia*. In a quest to raise profitability and short term reward, companies everywhere have been over-optimizing their business processes and ignoring an ancient planning truth: plan 80% with rigor and cunning, then leave 20% flexible for the Unpredictable. Scary stuff, because it requires reserving expensive resources that may end up not being used at all. Even worse, it may be abused in the most anti-operational horror known to process designers: improvisation.

Leadership teams grew blind to the fact the world around them is by nature unpredictable. They created a monster that leaves their business inflexible, unresponsive and in trouble. And the trouble accelerates, not just because of today's new economic reality, but for two systemic reasons as well.

- **Blinkered systems**. Masters of efficiency will be unaware they are in trouble until their relentlessly churning systems jam and it's way too late to correct course. Dell was the unrivalled master of assembling and delivering desktop computers to customized customer specification. But when the market interest abruptly shifted to laptops, Dell did not notice until stock started piling up in places it never had before. Had Dell been a little less 'perfect' on desktops and spent more resources on chasing (and failing) less profitable non-desktop market opportunities, it may have caught the laptop wave sooner. Similarly, the planet's most efficient manufacturing machine, Toyota, drove itself into unimaginable losses like a run-away train before it could tame the beast and adapt to the changed market dynamics.

- **Operator attitude**. The expertise required for Operational Excellence and the attitude required to successfully improvise are mutually exclusive. Businesses that accumulate pools of great process operators will naturally evolve into horrendous improvisers. And the more skewed resource pool, the more likely the one type will drive the other out of the organization as they tend to disagree on almost everything. So the better a business is equipped to accelerate profitability by Operational Excellence, the worse it will be at innovating and keeping an eye open for the next big opportunity. Just imagine what meetings are like in a room full of process operators once the systems have jammed. An operational mind-set tends to look for even further rigor in planning and stricter process controls, rather than questioning the output and the process itself.

Is there then no hope for Operational Excellence? Of course there is, and you can even dress up the solutions as old-school Operational Excellence so none of the accountants will notice. Here's what you do:

- **Fail faster**. Accelerating failure and dealing with regular small losses saves you from the life-threatening systemic bleeders. Do many small launches rather than few big ones. Ensure your production lines derail, jam or raise flags much faster when demand changes (even when it goes up). Operational Excellence systematically pushes business life into sameness, whilst it's the ability to notice, react to and create differences that help tap new opportunities.

Entrepreneurial attitude and incentives. In the micro-cosmos of Operational Excellence, the processes become more important than the output, which is reflected in employees' KPI's across all levels and disciplines. Marketing Managers are rewarded for concepts' performance in market research rather than on shelf. Manufacturing Managers receive applause for improving asset efficiency, but not for smart use of the resulting idle time when they optimize capacity beyond market demand. Customer Service teams are increasingly good at providing their customers help in ways prescribed in the helpdesk operation manuals, but hopeless when confronted with a non-scripted problem.

Perhaps I can summarize this as

Not a machine ...

... but a dynamic system.

Increasing flexibility, being less operationally excellent will appear like a short term dip in process efficiency. But finding a balance between planning and improvising is the only way to protect oneself long term from the Systemic Inertia that Operational Excellence naturally leads to.

"Our innovation programs always run on schedule" - person always ignoring unexpected & better ideas.

Innovation is 50% what you can do and 50% what you can get away with.

Delays imply quality issues as much as planning issues.

When things suddenly change, just hold on tight rather than try correcting it immediately – it could well just be turbulence.

The trouble with surprises is that they're unexpected. Particularly the ones you hadn't planned for.

The most popular idea is not necessarily the best one. Although that all depends on whether you're talking before or after launch.

Domain names are the new trademarks, but better.

If Operational Excellence and efficient use of resources were truly important, Heathrow and Gatwick would be the most reliable airports in the world.

Funny how quality stuff is worth maintaining whilst it's the crappy stuff that actually needs it.

Great prototypes are held together by duct tape and magic, poor ones by MS Project.

If things are not working out as planned, you may well have spent too much time planning.

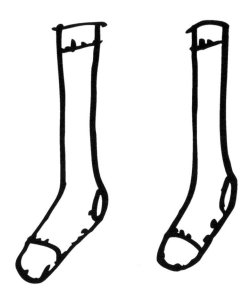

A SPARE PAIR OF LUCKY SOCKS
DOES NOT COUNT AS PLAN B

Is there a system or procedure for inventing new systems and procedures?

Funny how videoconferencing involves a lot more waving than any other type of meeting.

There is no such thing as 'unbalanced'. Only things that are balanced unfavourably to where you'd like them to be.

Of course, one possible explanation might be there is no explanation.

I hear it takes about five years to become an overnight success.

Pondering over two alternatives is just your conscious mind trying to convince your subconscious mind to reconsider.

That fact something is very unlikely doesn't mean it won't happen. Just like someone always wins the lottery, it's just unlikely to be you.

"Tried and Tested" methods are what one reaches for when in panic. Even when they've been proven to fail over and over. Habits die hard.

When asking yourself 'Is it feasible?' the key is understanding that it's as much about working on the 'it' as on the 'feasible'.

The devil is in the detail. Luckily, the divine is too.

In hindsight everything is obvious, including the inconceivable and the impossible.

Problems keep you occupied, solutions even more so.

Cutting costs is not a strategy, but being the cheapest is.

If new ideas required processes to be conceived, JFK would have said "before the end of the decade we will have NASA", not "a man on the moon".

Your market share growing from 90% to 91% may feel puny, but for the other player that meant 10% to 9% which has 10x the relative impact.

If gross margin were really as important as you think it is, your competitors wouldn't make you as nervous as you know you are.

Just like you avoid certain people because they kill your new ideas – they're avoiding you because you always congest their streamlined processes.

Value is remembered long after the price has been forgotten.

"Quick & Dirty Solution" - Funny how only the middle word carries any truth. Which is more than "Temporary Solution", where neither is true.

Growing pains - the fact you know it'll happen doesn't make it any less painful when you're in the middle of it. Like childbirth, probably.

Don't delude yourself into thinking you're discussing *what* you're going to do, when you're only talking about *how* you'll do it.

Paranoia, secrecy and speed to market are many times more effective than any patent can ever be.

Hey marketing managers: When did you last consider your factories an asset, rather than an obstacle?

Airport security must be the only place in the world where "oh just randomly" is considered a good reason for doing something.

Don't mistake "potential" for "value", they're on different time lines.

Hey, if you don't like the way we run this metro, go take one in another town.

YES MA'AM, I KNOW YOU PUT OUT THE FIRE. I JUST WANT TO MAKE SURE IT YOU DID IT ACCORDING TO DIN4102-22.

Of course, once it's perfect, it still needs a lot of improvement.

Innovation success levels are best raised by raising caffeine levels first.

Whatever your MBA mind may tell you, in innovation a straight line is much less effective than a meandering one.

Calculating ROI on a one sentence concept is like suggesting to get married on a first date: in some cultures it's perfectly acceptable.

The simplest problems can spin out of control if you take time to think about them.

As long as the majority of the Western world calls vegetables "rabbit food" there's no chance of us all living to be 100.

Ambiguity doesn't fare well in an operational world, but a creative context, I'm afraid it's essential.

"2 + 2 = 4", regardless of culture, religion or political stance. But it does assume you've agreed using a base-10 counting protocol.

Versatile and Efficient are mutually exclusive. Whatever the business book promises, you can't excel at both.

Fancy hotel rooms - there's always one light you can't find the switch for.

Any debate as to where 'breaking point' lies is hypothetical until it actually breaks. Before then, it's mere emotions in conversation.

Breakthrough graphic design drives trial, not repeat. Breakthrough product design drives repeat, not trial. So you still need to do both.

Don't call things "barriers" just because you haven't done them before.

> **Don't walk into anything you can't walk away from. That goes for cave exploration, Sao Paulo by night and procurement negotiations.**

ERP, MRP, systems & procedures automation: the different types of databases available to structure your countless Excel sheets.

If you're not complaining about the pain in the arse that innovation is most of the time, you're not innovating properly.

"As seen on TV" - just so you know, because you probably didn't see it.

Insisting on having breakthrough ideas AND a fixed development budget is like insisting on having kids AND French nails.

If you want people to smile when hearing of your new product, consider naming it the TinkyWillyStrudel instead of the RX2000i.

Hey experts - are you merely distinguishing the insane from the feasible or are you making the insane feasible?

In some categories, retail price is still defined by cost of materials. What do you call one notch below "commodity"?

"Extended Offer!!" - sells poorly, even at reduced price

It seems the phrase "more likely than not" is too often interpreted as "100% definitely yes". At least more often than not.

Modern cars are ultra-safe for crash test dummies. Yet people still get killed. Your model is not reality.

Competitors under-pricing you, use their profits to increase quality. Which gives you TWO problems, not one.

It's all about the deatils.

If you innovate your way into trouble, you need good operational skills to get out. And vice versa.

Whatever factory you visit, regardless of what they produce, always compliment the floor manager on his/her choice of raw materials.

"August 12th. Great, it's almost Christmas." – half of all retail teams, anywhere.

If anyone objects to, or doubts the quality of your big new idea... distract them by starting a hair-splitting discussion on the meaning of the word "innovation".

If you've come to present the outcomes of a project, no one's eager to hear all about the process first.

How come Planning Meetings always overrun?

**REMARKABLY, THE REAL THING
IS NO WHERE NEAR AS BAD AS
IT IS ON PAPER.**

More advertising for a failing product is like speaking louder to a person who speaks another language, hoping to be understood.

Like children, ideas will eventually grow up and walk out into the world on their own. But not before having gone through puberty with you

"There are 7 fundamental ways of organizing a business. Yet over 50% of the companies out there don't follow any of them" - Idiot with an MBA.

Step 1 to bringing down product cost is cranking up volume, not finding cheaper parts.

If you're spending more time honing the pre-amble than the idea, don't even try launching it. Find another place to work.

The money your consumer saved from that discount you gave will be spent on something else that isn't discounted, not on you.

Countries that shut down in August work 1/12th harder the rest of the year, right?

Some rooms are cool, good for meetings. Other rooms are hot, good for Bikram Yoga. The two are not compatible.

"Deja Due" - the illusion of having missed a deadline before it's actually passed.

Always check before using a file labelled 'Final' by colleagues. There may well be one labelled 'Final4' or 'FinalReleased' out there too.

Just because it looks good in Excel doesn't mean it's good in the real world.

Successful new products and services are a bit like the weather; about 70% identical to yesterday's products.

There's no point debating your portfolio strategy if you have only one product. Seriously.

Remember back when stuff only looked good on paper, you at least had some paper? Now It's only looking good on *.pptx, if you're lucky.

Product launch is not the endpoint of an innovation process. It's at best the halfway point.

Things that are difficult to dispose of: nuclear waste, conscience, children, reputation, dreams, CO_2, MRSA and childhood Lego.

"Western population is growing fatter and fatter" - finally some good news for our ailing pension funds.

When you introduce an innovative process, at least reserve some budget for the poor guy/gal who has to rewrite all your ISO9001 certificates.

Corporate ideation birth chambers are, like any birth chamber, quite messy.

So your ISO9001 procedure describes innovation as a yearly workshop with a madman in a Hawaiian shirt shouting 'great idea' all day long?

Visibility on shelf is important, indeed. But not as important as being visible in the place your product is supposed to be used.

"Buy One, Get One Free" - our sales KPIs are on volume, not margin. And we don't have a clue what you'd pay full price for.

The difference between running projects and ruining projects can be as little as a 1-letter typo.

Then again, the unsung benefit of a totally miserable innovation process is that everyone will want to get over with it quickly.

The Chicago L track... Certainly someone must have interrupted the structural design phase asking: "Are we all sure steel isn't too noisy?"

I would like to suggest using broccoli to coat the next generation of orbit & re-entry space shuttles. Nothing cools faster than broccoli.

A webcam adds 10 pounds. So there's some innovation necessary before women will allow video conferencing to become the new standard.

Only few things explode when the pressure rises too high. Most things just crack and start leaking. Sorry, I meant humans.

"Now 30% off" – now 0% off, but we think you won't notice.

The price is almost never too high. It's usually the value which is too low.

Note that the people who populate the Gantt charts confuse "check promising alternative" with "delay". Don't even try to explain.

Whatever manufacturing principle you're considering, there's only a very thin line between lean & mean and malnourished.

"The Schmeeting Point" - the point when more time is spent in meetings discussing what to do, than the time spent doing what is discussed.

Is there a process for being result-focused?

Step 1 in improving efficiency is building trust, not process control. Simply because it allows you to scrap meetings and reviews.

"Who would like to join our committee to discuss ways of reducing non-value-add operational projects and processes?"

Breakthrough innovation is about resolving category barriers, not your own manufacturing limitations.

Failure Mode & Effect Analysis overviews tend to cover technology assessment only. I bet FMEA's were invented by a commercial team. #Irony

THE PLANT

6σ OFFICES

The secret to tracking less noise & error is tracking less.

"Limited Offer" - one warehouse full to be precise and we're never ever going to run a batch of this disaster product again.

If you need to update your MS Project Gantts daily, you are not planning. You're merely recording the past - and wasting your time.

Whether or not it's a comeback depends on where you peg the reference point. But 20% gain after a 60% drop is *never* a comeback.

Contracts and signed agreements: if they are written properly, they stay tucked away in the drawer forever.

Don't plan prototypes through your MRP system. Unless it can handle a Bill Of Material with only two parts, duct tape and magic.

The Cost-of-Goods delusion. Cheaper ingredients lead to lower quality leads to lower volume leads to higher cost. Higher volume lowers cost.

Wishful thinking is fine, up to the moment that reality presents itself.

Measuring and controlling are too often confused as meaning the same.

That fact it appears disorganised doesn't automatically mean it is inefficient or unproductive.

Has your Lean/6σ VP suggested ways to make his/her own team obsolete yet? I thought so.

Don't change a winning formula? My impression is winning formulas contain less and less formula over time.

Process efficiency implies *less* process, not more.

Dear Operational Excellence manager, there's no point boasting improved asset efficiency if the excess capacity isn't used making something else.

An innovation process that has become part of your operational structure is as flawed as an operational process that is re-invented continuously.

[**Nothing is impossible.
It's just that some things
are bloody expensive.**]

Feasibility issues? You mean CapEx and Cost Of Goods issues. Which you should have dealt with up front.

Shipping more air with your new 'mousse' food product to save cost? Why not go all the way? Inflate it at shelf and save on logistics too.

Don't be fooled by political barriers being presented as technical barriers.

If you only have a clipper, every problem seems like a nail.

Market Research
& Modelling Madness

**HONESTLY? I THINK IT TASTES LIKE
DOG'S TESTICLES. BUT I'M SURE IT'S
WHAT CONSUMERS WANT BECAUSE WE CO-
CREATED IT WITH 15,000 OF THEM
ACROSS 12 MARKETS.**

Market Research
& Modelling Madness

Corporate market research is mostly a rational process, whilst people are mostly emotionally driven. That discrepancy exists because people may well act on whims, but you can't run a business on whims. At least not officially.

Hence 'market knowledge' comes in the rational form of market research departments that feed market & consumer data into the other parts of the business. Statisticians with huge brains populate this area, applying big mathematics and promising us true understanding of what's going on in the big bad world outside the company walls. They can show what rational and emotional drivers are making your market happen. It's like having an oracle in your back room and it can be all too tempting to let the data make the decisions for you instead of merely informing them.

When you operate in mass markets, it is in practice impossible to talk to all of your potential 1×10^x ($x \gg 3$) customers. The business needs prompt and cheap access to answers – particularly in fast moving, competitive environments. Luckily, statisticians offer us shortcuts: *samples*. If you just ask a few hundred people for an opinion, their answers will be representative for the opinions of the whole population.

Not.

> **Research data is skewed**. *People have ninja level skills when it comes to sneaking past research recruiters. Whether it's clipboard guys in supermarkets, call centres or online surveys, the feedback they collect is*

skewed towards the part of the population too polite to say "sorry – I'm not interested".

- **Joe Average may not have much to say.** *In the context of innovation, querying average consumers will get you average answers. Even heavy users don't necessarily engage with their products. The fact you run your dishwasher twice a day doesn't mean you have anything interesting to say about dishwasher tablets. Of course there are people out there with profound, avant-garde views on dishwashing – but they're not average and they don't live in typical research panels.*

- **Receiving answers to questions doesn't mean you're asking the right questions.** *We all love asking lotsa questions, it gives us mortals a sense of getting closer to the truth. But curious researchers often overlook that real people simply don't know all the details the researcher would love to uncover. They remember incorrectly if they had two beers with their spaghetti Bolognese last month or three colas with their hamburger. But most people are nice, gentle souls and they'll give you an answer either way. And they'll do so even quicker after 30 minutes of ploughing through a tedious survey.*

- **Developed to 'test well'.** *Probably the biggest problem of follows from all of the above: the tendency of research to be institutionalized in tollgate decision making. Rather than removing the risk of launching the wrong products, it leads to a mind-set of creating propositions that do well in tests rather than in market. Endless honing and word-smithing of identical concepts just to get them to score above go/no-go* *thresholds instead of picking the right direction from a batch of distinguishable alternatives.*

Is it all hopeless and is market research useless? Of course not. Keep in mind this is not about day-to-day operational stuff, like measuring the efficacy of a commercial or how well you're doing in comparison to a competitor. The context I'm describing is that of *innovation*, a fuzzy world with far less clarity for respondents to hold on to, simply because they're being asked to comment about products that do not yet exist. Even the most elaborate concept description and usage storyboard will require a respondent to *imagine* what it's like to use the product or service. That's difficult. This means the normal statistical rules around sampling do not apply, human error sits in the way too much. One cannot ask even the savviest consumer to rank a feeling of "Dunno, maybe I'd try" on a 5-point Lickert scale and expect an accurate response. Nor will refining the options to a 10-point scale make the outcome any more precise, no matter what maths you unleash upon it.

Then what to do with research for innovation? Face-to-face qualitative research can only carry so far; there will come a moment you and your colleagues at risk management will want some cover from bigger numbers.

- **Talk to the right people**. *Once you've realized most respondent panels are skewed, you may as well bend it in your favour. Filter for the category Lead Users [von Hippel 1986]. About 5-10% of any category's consumers show a significantly higher interest for improvements from that category. They're frustrated, try and tinker with product variations and simply have a much deeper need for progress from brands and companies like yours. They're almost always one step ahead of the masses' category behaviour, just what you need. But be aware* *this is category-led and not personality-led. Lead users have more interest in a few categories, not all of them. I'm a lead user of yoghurts myself, but couldn't care less about custards.*

Be comfortable with being ROUGHLY right. *Just like censorship is often self-applied, most precision is demanded by people doing their own measurements. Moving in the right direction is much more valuable than spending forever trying to precisely measure something that does not yet exist. And because you keep moving, you can enjoy the relaxedness of doing sequential batches of small research rather than one big budget-guzzling piece that has the future of the business – or at least your career – depending on it.*

Forget about early adopters. *These people tend to be mere shopaholics and everyone who buys a lot will get lucky and be 'on trend' more often than normal mortals.*

Stay away from brand lovers. *Once they've calmed down from the excitement that someone working for their favourite brand is asking them questions, they aren't very likely to give you valuable critique as to what you're up to for future launches. Would you offer valuable feedback to someone you are madly in love with?*

Be cautious with generalizations. *Someone once pointed me to the fact the average consumer has one tit and one testicle. Statistically 100% true – and 100% useless. To get insight into the lives and drivers of millions of people, a degree of generalization will always be necessary. Using consumer 'personas' is an example of using such shortcuts, but they can lead down a tricky path. Not because the underlying statistics aren't sound, but because personas tend to become a catch-all for very* *elementary human drivers (think Maslow) without relevant context of a particular situation. And it's those situational settings that provide the best base for creating innovative products. With only personas and their abstract motivations to go on, context will be extrapolated on the spot – "Oh, I think Helga The Hunter-Gatherer would really love this". And then we're in fantasy land.*

Paraphrasing the brilliant philosopher Alfred Korzibsky:

Your model ...

... is NOT reality.

No matter how much love and care you put into creating it, no matter how great it would be if the model were 100% accurate, it never is. In the context of innovation, trust your model only to inform your decisions but *never* let it make the decisions for you.

Speaking of male chauvinism, the pilot on my flight home was a real character. She said we all think in stereotypes.

Opinions will do just fine as long as the truth is unclear. Just don't confuse the two, please.

Beware of the mischievous bell curve, its tails are fatter than you think. And it may be more pointy. Actually it may not be bell shaped at all.

"Wisdom of crowds"? On average, everyone in the hippodrome loses at the races. "Wisdom of the bookies" is a better inspiration for strategy.

Would you have rated a high Purchase Intent score for all the kitchen appliances (men) and shoes (women) you have in the house? Be honest.

"And that, my friends, is the truth" - market researcher's famous last words

A 2nd opinion is just that: an opinion. You choose what your truth will be. How very metaphysical.

"We're doing our very best to help stranded passengers with food, drink and free WiFi" - Maslow needs revision.

Keep in mind that consumer drivers in the UK and Japan drive on the wrong side of the road.

Confidence driven by facts and confidence driven by statistics are not the same. But you can pretend it is, as no one seems to have noticed this yet.

Knowing the n=150 fish in your aquarium really well doesn't mean you can predict fish behaviour in all of the Atlantic.

Try completing one of your own surveys first before complaining about drop-out rates.

The more you interpret the data, the further you dwell from the truth, by definition. Your beautiful map is not reality.

When creating a need segmentation study, please segment along customer needs or occasions. Not along your company's organizational chart.

'Science' means looking for falsification, not more proof you're right.

With obesity and poverty expanding globally at the rates they do... isn't predicting today's new-borns will all live to be 100 rather naive?

If you're struggling to uncover clear needs, cast a narrower net. It's easier finding bankable kitchen needs than home needs than life needs.

Remember the days when "the data" would answer your business questions for you?

Ask yourself: 'revealed' versus 'declared' consumer behaviour... Which is best at uncovering opportunities and which are you using now?

**HEY, DON'T SNEAK UP ON ME
LIKE THAT, WILL YA?**

By definition, the population sample that's representative for your next opportunity is not representative for the current status quo.

Opportunities without risk only exist in the past. If you see a future opportunity without risk, brace yourself for surprises.

Topping the menu in most bars is their free WiFi, not their food & drink. Just like my ISP offers coupons for pizza delivery deals.

When creating a vision, emphasis on market research will ensure your case is history-proof, not future-proof.

Trendspotting and trainspotting have a lot more in common than just the binoculars, cameras, newsletters, clipboards and eleven letters.

If you knew what to look for, you wouldn't need to look. At least make sure to know why you're looking before worrying where to look.

Keep in mind that historical benchmarks are exactly that: historical. They predict concept performance in case you launched last year.

Not understanding your consumer's motivations is a mutual experience. He/she thinks you're odd too.

If you're looking for experts on near future developments, talk to a bookie. Unlike market researchers, their livelihood depends on correct predictions.

**IF YOU DON'T LIKE MY TRENDS,
I HAVE MORE WHERE THESE
CAME FROM!**

Statistical outliers... maybe it's important, maybe it's a fat finger, maybe it's someone joking around with the clipboard guy.

Privacy is like health, you don't really miss until it you lose it. Teenagers care equally little about both.

Sending out ever more surveys to raise confidence usually means distributing them amongst ever less ideal respondents.

Trend watching... The poor man's trend setting.

If your futurologist is surprised you called, find a better one.

Continental drift is a highly predictable macro trend, but quite tough to use as inspiration for new concepts.

Empathy for your consumers doesn't mean that if you like a concept they automatically will too.

Hey market researchers: don't worry about finding the truth. In the end it will find you.

Market Research is a great for predicting the past.

Segmentation 'personas' all too often sound like stereotypes from a cheesy TV sitcom. Which explains the cliché results generated by using them.

The more you need an answer, the fewer questions you ask. And vice versa.

An opinion carried by crowds does not make it more correct. Unless they're also carrying pitchforks and torches.

"4 in 5 market research studies are pretty much useless", says 1 in 5 market researchers.

A 2% difference in scores between only two concepts means respondents:
A- are deeply polarized
B- can't see the difference
C- don't care.

It cannot be a coincidence that 'quantitative market research' anagrams to 'heart attack via requirements'.

When futurologists say 'because'... be very cautious. When historians say 'because', be even more sceptical.

Clues proving you cannot be wrong are much stronger than those showing you're right.

Funny how the extrapolated extension of 'truth' is 'insight', whereas the extrapolated appendix of 'lies' is 'statistics'.

Whoever feels stuck with abstract personas as target consumer descriptions, ought to come to the IKEA canteen. Everyone 'real' is here.

"This morning in the supermarket, I had 72% intent to purchase this product" - no one, ever.

AND FINALLY, AFTER THREE HOURS OF
INTERVIEWING, THE RESPONDENT SAID SHE
JUST WANTED THE OLD MODEL TO BE
CHEAPER.

AND THEN I KILLED HER,
YOUR HONOR.

Whenever a futurologist or trend analyst defends past predictions with a sentence starting "if it weren't for...", walk away.

If you're handing out incentives to respondents for any answer they give, why not award prizes for the right answer?

Yo Momma innovates so bad, she brought her own sample to the market research team, in a cup.

Correlation and Causation only differ when you care enough about the topic.

Hey market researchers, enough with the fancy tools OK? Great painters aren't admired for their brushes either. Well, except Bob Ross maybe.

Which one of your trademarked personas are you yourself? Let me guess, you're a mix of at least three of them?

Robo-moderator algorithm: ECHO("Tell me about (Topic$)") THEN LOOP(3;"Why do you say that" OR "tell me more") THEN RANDOM("rank this"; END).

Depending on paid respondents for market research is like walking into a red light district to find true love. Real, but not authentic.

Whomever got the Dualit toaster through concept testing and prototyping deserves the World Spin Award.

How innovative! This focus group facility has doubled the viewing room behind the mirror for use as a sauna!

Yo Momma's so fat she skews every sample she ends up in.

Unlike reading reports, you can have new ideas while you sleep. Now who's being efficient, eh?

Some topics simply cannot be made into a science, no matter how badly you want to sound scientific. No control group? No science.

Paraphrasing Mother Theresa: "If I research the masses, I'm paralyzed by pie-charts. If I listen to individuals, I'm inspired to innovate".

Testing a concept without its Umfeld on shelf is no different from buying a house without considering the neighbourhood.

$(TREND)^2$ = the habit of trend watchers to parrot other trend watchers instead of observing populations.

Yo Momma's so bad at market research she thought a respondent pool was for people wearing Speedos and swimming goggles.

Research the idea until the risk has gone and you'll find the opportunity has disappeared along with it.

Only in market research are we happy to take advice from total strangers.

We found a way to measure 100% accurate Purchase Intent and it involves baby unicorns.

HOW ODD – ACCORDING TO YOUR DEMOGRAPHIC PROFILES YOU SHOULD HAVE THOUGHT THAT WAS INCREDIBLY FUNNY.

I think the best way to moderate a focus group is to pretend you're Oprah Winfrey for 2x 45 minutes.

It's not the volume of data that counts, but the amount of sleep you get to process the little bit of important data.

Funnelvision: If the focus group doesn't like your idea, re-recruit and re-test 'till it passes.

Offering multiple choice answers is a sign you don't know what question to ask.

* SPOILER ALERT *
A USP in no way guarantees actual selling.

I am at this very moment experiencing a very niche consumer need for on-the-go stain remover. In particular for molten Mozzarella stains.

If you ask lapsed users why they left, OF COURSE they will say it was because of price. They're too nice to tell you the truth.

Be smart in a downward economy and halve your market research recruitment costs through respondents with split personality disorder.

Somewhere, a marketing manager is planning new products based on a persona just like you.

Input: 24x observations, 8x opinionated session participants and 46x verbatim, how many insight permutations does that lead to?

Did you do your due diligence and check with consumers or did you check with consumers to do your due diligence? – Not the same.

How many of the consumers from your last co-creation session would you hire as Product Development Manager? Then use their input accordingly.

Yo Momma's so fat she can make n=1 volumetric modeling credible.

"Cleaning the Data", aka "Censoring".

THOSE OUTLIERS ARE MAKING ME NERVOUS TOO, BUT I SUGGEST WE IGNORE THEM JUST FOR NOW, OK?

You can predict next year's trends with 90% accuracy by copying last year's trends. Which shows how 90% accurate can be 100% useless.

Why use the Large Hadron Collider? I know market research departments creating datasets large enough to reveal the Higgs Boson every week.

People are even lazier than they are vain.

When was the last time you did a reality-check on your Excel-sheet driven strategy? And quant research doesn't count as 'reality'.

Don't mix statistics with catch-all terminology. "62.4% want Eco-friendly products" doesn't mean ANYthing.

Statistically, there's no difference between you throwing the dice or a stranger doing it for you. Now tell me you're not superstitious and let me throw for you.

Yo Momma's so fat, she's her own mass market.

When people speak of 'dynamic' lifestyles, they often mean the opposite: 'turbulent'. An active way of standing still.

There are two types of people; those who leave OEM stickers all over their laptops and cameras, and those who don't understand these people.

In the simplified reality of market research, the difference between good and bad is merely a question of benchmarks.

Somewhere, the folks marketing products you love, talk about you & your habits with the same simpleton tone you talk about your consumers.

Decision making: when entering new terrain, a compass will outperform any map. Particularly one created behind a desk.

"Significance levels? The Consumer Truth? What I'm revealing here is your FATE!" - Balsy market researcher pushing the envelope.

A market research report presented as a story is very compelling. But remember the ugly reality has no plot, no narrative, no climax, no ending.

"So if everyone starts jumping off a cliff, you'd do too then?!"
- If your parent is a trend watcher, the answer they want to hear is "Yes".

It seems modern market research machismo all boils down to who has the biggest data.

"Concept Screening" anagrams to "Connecting Creeps" - remember, you heard it here first.

Yo Momma's so fat, analysts call her when they need Big Data.

Ask a consumer for an opinion and they'll give you one. Not because they have an opinion, but because you asked for one.

Trend reports are like weather reports, sending everyone to the same, overcrowded sunny beaches. Real value is spotting the rain ahead.

I hear Neuro MR is so expensive it sits in the CFO's budget.

If numerologists can 'predict' Kennedy's murder from the Bible, imagine the nonsense you can 'mine' from 1.7Tb of consumer data.

You'll have to accept - and defend - that "maybe" is sometimes the best possible answer.

Re-framing 'stereotyping' as 'segmentation study' must be the market research industry's greatest PR stunt to date.

The middle word in "insight" is "sigh".

If alien civilizations would read a typical FMCG research report, their first conclusion would be humans stop buying stuff at the age of 49.

Best-Sellers, Fiction, Non-Fiction, Business, Science, Children and Self-Help. The sections in a typical FMCG segmentation study report.

The best crystal balls don't look into the future, but selectively regurgitate stuff from the past.

Great project prank to mess up your colleague's concept scores: add "with free coupons" to the worst concept's benefit statement.

"I don't know" - is a message seldom delivered with the clarity it deserves.

Big Data isn't new. Just check pages 3 to 467 of your research report. It's all there.

I wonder if religious people see the irony of most atheists ALSO completely mixing up causation and correlation.

Statistical significance vs financial significance: when market research is SO expensive that the outcomes simply have to be true.

Unless you work in office furniture design, there's little chance you do decent consumer research sitting at your desk.

Yo Momma's so fat she's a heavy user in every category.

* SPOILER ALERT * The €500K segmentation study you just commissioned will reveal an axis labelled ME-WE and claim that is very relevant.

Yesterday I had a vodka; then wrote three concepts and filed my taxes. The concepts bombed but my tax man scored top-2 purchase intent.

I have a hunch that SPSS was originally coded by Uri Geller. And then debugged by Houdini.

Just like gold mining, data mining unearths mostly gravel and fossils.

NO, I DON'T GET IT. YOU SAID YOU WANTED A POOL OF RESPONDENTS.

"I understand you're not comfy in that MRI scanner and you'd rather go home, but this is costing us $60K a day so shut up" - Neuro MR

Statistical analysis is about interpreting what you observed, not bridging the gap to what you hoped were true & think is right.

"Tell me a little more... WHY should I take the garbage out?" - Focus group moderator heading for trouble by taking work behaviours home.

FACT: Beware of trend spotters talking about 'facts'.

If you diligently dig through all 380 pages of a typical quant research report, you'll eventually reach the arse it was meant to cover.

"CONFESS!! NOW TALK, YOU B*STARD!!" - Market researcher interrogating the data.

When you're desperate for good news, n=1 is suddenly good enough.

Brand managers talking about loving their consumers - it says more about their perception of love than of their relationship with consumers.

What's more convincing? A market researcher with a PhD or one who has QUAL & QUANT tattooed on his knuckles?

Paradox: 'laziness' is a consumer driver.

Sometimes focus group outputs are so spot on strategy, you'd wonder if the mirror wasn't mounted the wrong way around.

If you layer 3 consumer frameworks on top of each other, you'll never need to talk to a real person again to make your Excel forecast work.

We needed idiot-proof concepts, so we ran a co-creation session with a bunch of statistically representative idiots.

Market research is not meant to reduce risk, but to navigate it. To help & support your decisions, not to make them for you.

Remember that only the summary slide of your 423 page report will survive and lead a life of its own. The reasoning will vanish.

"... And to really get to the bottom of it, we need to do more market research." - the final sentence of 99% of market research reports.

Decision Making Along The S-Curve

**YOUR OTHER IDEAS WERE ALL CULLED IN
ACCORDANCE TO MY KPI'S.**

Decision Making AlongThe S-Curve

Dynamic systems – be it people, businesses or products –
evolve roughly according to an S-curve.

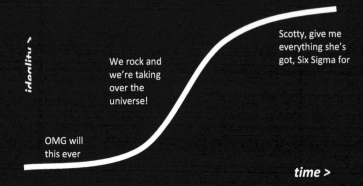

This flow across three main stages (infancy, growth,
maturity) has been common understanding for at least half
a century, probably much longer. And here's a funny thing I
noticed whilst searching for representations of S-curves
online:

A) When they're used to describe *business* growth,
they're usually stacked like this:

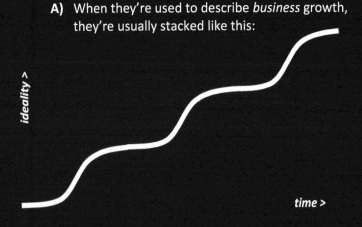

B) But when describing *technology* evolution, they are stacked quite differently:

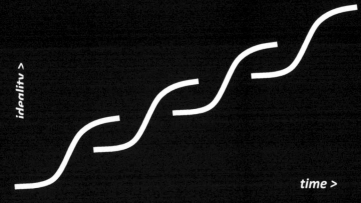

The difference is obviously the way they connect. **A)** is all about good news, whilst **B)** shows that whatever new curve kicks off, there will be a lapse in ideality (=efficiency) when you transition.

In case you're wondering, **B)** is the correct one. Libraries could be filled with case studies of companies sliding into oblivion because they couldn't switch to the new technology for no other reason than it would kill their short term profitability along with their cash cow. This is why game changers are *almost* never introduced by market leaders. When they do, it requires an existential crisis.

Which brings us to the topic of decision making. Taking a truly grumpy view on this, we can assume that human decisions will always be made with the best interest of that particular Human in mind. In a business environment with a proper hierarchy in place, this is then less about decisions and more about offering scenarios to the next person upstream that will make the Human look good:

- **High reward.** *Acting in best interest of the business, generating growth, everyone achieves their KPI's.*

- **Low risk.** *Doing the above with least risk, resource or cost within the period the Human is expected to be in his/her current role.*

With this perception of human nature in mind, it's pretty obvious that ignorance or denial of what the next evolutionary phase holds in store will lead to 'good news' - and a severly blinkered view on what scenarios are best for the business.

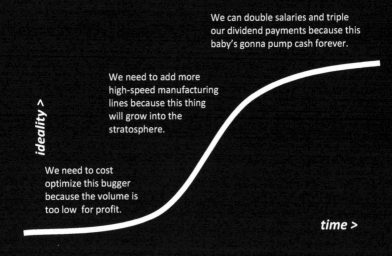

We can double salaries and triple our dividend payments because this baby's gonna pump cash forever.

We need to add more high-speed manufacturing lines because this thing will grow into the stratosphere.

ideality >

We need to cost optimize this bugger because the volume is too low for profit.

time >

Is this too harsh? Is this just another plea for longer term KPI's and rewards for management? Partially. For an innovative corporate culture to grow sustainably, it must reward decisions that ensure the business is future-proof, because business reality will have changed by the time scenarios trickle down into action:

- *When your expensive, rattling prototypes show promise they might actually work: start building them in a low-*

volume and flexible pilot setup rather than waiting for the perfection necessary to produce them on expensive high-speed assets.

- *When recruiting new team members, assume the business will have evolved and grown by the time they're in place.*

- *When production capacity starts to max out, don't simply install a copy of your existing manufacturing line but build one you can more easily re-tool for the next generation when demand goes down again – which it will.*

Setting KPI's to entice such future-proofing mean they should reward not what would be great *now*, but what would facilitate evolving to the next phase of your business. None of this is rocket science, yet it seems a struggle for small and large businesses alike.

It's no different from raising children. You don't buy clothes that fit snugly now, you buy things they will grow into soon. You look ahead, because you *know* they'll grow.

What this boils down to?

Planning for success ...

... is planning for transition.

1853, Elisha Otis. I wonder where he pitched his idea for the elevator.

Most decision makers need to see a few options first, before they can say "no".

Show me five good reasons not to progress a new idea and I'll show you at least ten better ones.

The pyramids weren't built top-down either.

If you're hoping for things to get better, they will definitely get worse first. Hope is not a strategy.

It's a shame you can't recover the black box after a failed market launch.

The guys on the other side of the fence are busy genetically engineering greener grass right now.

When you're confronted with a stunning competitive market introduction, "how did they do that?" is the least of your worries.

Once you've achieved "perfection", the next stage is "promising alternative".

Live like there's no tomorrow - a guarantee to remain stuck in yesterday.

I wonder what happens when this tsunami of Y-Gens suddenly all realize they're not geniuses and just as mediocre as us X-Gens before them?

Any idea is only as good as the length of time to find a better one. Hopefully it'll be yours again.

You can't blame the other person for being tolerated.

Most business books on succeeding in innovation forget to mention "Willingness to work Saturdays and Sundays".

Funny things happen when young marketing managers take over a brand and aren't aware what part of the brand history was truth and what was spin.

Bigger and Badder: If your EPD threshold is being just about acceptable in comparison to last year's EPD, you'll end up with a shitty product.

Only Generation-Y truly understand the importance of Lady Gaga as a cultural phenomenon. Only Generation-X understand both need to grow up.

"Get straight to the periphery of the problem" seems to be the preferred approach in today's innovation teams.

If you're wondering what innovation to launch next, just ask yourself what would be your worst nightmare for a competitor to launch.

Head in the sand or head in the clouds, both make you neck hurt.

Pushing new ideas through an organization: the pain is definitely real. Shame that the cause usually isn't.

Best way to learn implementing breakthrough innovation: implement not-so-breakthrough innovation first and see where the system pushes back.

When was it that we all started assuming there's a simple solution to every problem, regardless of its complexity?

On your quest for the person who can say 'yes' to your idea, you'll meet many who can say 'no' first. Make friends to make it happen.

For innovators with a large sophisticated toolbox, every problem becomes a complex multi-disciplinary challenge. Sometimes hammers are good.

"Yes, of course your innovation program will throw up a hurdle. Now stop whining and get over it".

Decision making on gut instinct may save us time and the bore of post-rationalization, but it doesn't mean it's less prone to error.

When weighing pro's and con's, be aware that the con's are in reality inversed pro's of alternatives you haven't yet considered.

Milestones' and 'Tollgates' are a managerial invention. Reality is fluid.

There are always more reasons in favour of holding another meeting than there are for scrapping an existing one. Like with government legislation.

Insisting on first-time-right innovation -without detours- is like urging to paddle when you could be sailing. More tiring and much slower.

Check if your Risk Management Advisor ties double knots in his/her shoelaces. If not, walk away.

Just like one creates solutions step-by-step and not instantly, one might as well throw up problems one-by-one rather than all at once.

Balancing 'Time', 'Cost' & 'Quality' in any project is like a game of Whack-The-Mole. Bring in 'Politics' to keep them all above ground.

Big ideas sometimes need to be dressed up as small ones, just to survive company politics and decision making procedures.

Conflicts exist where you choose not to walk away. But walk away too soon and you'll find the conflict comes with you as a moral dilemma.

When two opinions clash, it's usually not the opinions that matter but their owners. Compromises save face, solutions make partners.

Maybe successful innovation really is no more than just doing what everyone else is thinking?

GRRRRREAT PRODUCT. IS THERE A WAY WE
CAN CONNECT IT TO OUR FACEBOOK PAGE?

CONSUMERS LOVE FACEBOOK YOU KNOW.

The typical number of bridges between FMCG Marketing and Manufacturing teams is either none or one too far.

Inertia is not an external factor stopping you. Nor is paralysis.

"You're one in a million" sounds so much nicer than "there are only about 6,500 other people just like you".

**Innovation decisions: one path takes you to endless hard work, missed holidays and possibly divorce.
The other path takes you to failure.**

You can't blame poor innovators for the fact they have so many other important meetings to attend.

How come time slows down the closer you get to your destination? Unless your destination is a deadline.

Urgent, important, critical. Three words meaning entirely different things, yet so often mixed up. Even by smart people.

Stakeholders who have nothing to win/lose are not stakeholders. They're just nosy, bossy or simply bored and they should be kept at distance.

The sun's energy for 1 minute can power the world for a year. Yeah. And all the water in the sea can quench humanity's thirst for eternity.

Sunday evening is the new Monday morning.

In an ideal world, mistakes have 'rewind' buttons to undo the damage. On the other hand, a crisis needs a 'fast forward'.

The journey from problem to solution can resemble a game of Chinese Whispers. Only without the laughter at the end.

When you're really hungry, even crap food tastes delicious. Same story when you're starving for new ideas. Don't ideate on an empty funnel.

Brand lovers are about as good a judge about the brand as anyone who is head-over-heels in love.

 "No, I don't see the irony at all", replied the trend spotter who kept on whining about the current tough market for trend spotting agencies.

Are smartphones making me dumber? They must be.

> **When you reach the end of the page in your notebook, it coincidentally always feels like you've made just about enough notes.**

Naivety is one of the most expensive talents to be blessed with.

You can fake workshop energy levels - but you can't fake innovation success.

"I really wish this brand offered me a more diverse, richer portfolio experience" - not a single consumer, ever.

Reminder: you do *not* need twice the number of line extensions on shelf to double your brand's revenue.

If you have to be convinced by a metric that you're successful, then you probably aren't.

Tightly defined innovation processes not only exclude the necessity for getting lucky, they prevent any chance of it happening entirely.

> **Whether you bet on Plan A or Plan B, you only ever get Result A.**

Whatever attracted your consumer, will also pull them away. Win on price, lose on price. Ensure your differentiating benefit lasts.

Runaway successes need good shoes, not business planning.

When scoping your project: remember that you, your team, your boss and your boss' bosses are not the people actually buying your product.

Every innovation success story has this moment where the "can we please speed up" attitude switches to "for god sake slow down please".

Innovation is as much about knowing what to ignore as what to follow.

No, most personalities are not layered like onions. More like eggs. Crack the thin civilized shell and the messy insides come running out.

Every innovation team has an Axl Rose who walks out on tedious jobs and a Slash who can't finish his solos.

Corporate navel gazing also involves lots of fluff.

Somewhere, right now, someone's considering advertising their business in a phone book.

You can't buy momentum, sadly. Nor a trend.

Claiming you're "living on the edge" says less about the "edge" and more about what you call "living".

Poor quality coffee makes me really opinionated about just about everything.

Good news always comes in pairs; mostly because the high of the first one influences your judgment for a while. Ditto for bad news.

If you get no reaction, your action is the problem (Newton's 3rd).

Compromises eventually catch up with you, being something neither of you wanted.

Is there a way to make a scattered, granular organization work as one harmonious entity (like a beehive) without sounding like a hippie?

Under the right circumstances, a university degree and PhD in molecular science can be trumped by 6 evening classes on PowerPoint skills.

Of course, if the outlook is bleak - you can always indulge in the cocoon of wishful thinking.

If you give something away for free, the money your 'client' saves won't come your way later. It'll go somewhere else that isn't free, now.

It's the simple stuff that is complex to come up with.

It takes two to polarize.

Marketing disasters don't need more marketing to be undone.

Opportunitanosmia - the inability to smell an opportunity
Paradox: Consumers act mostly on whims, but you can't run a business on whims. Or at least you can't publicly acknowledge you do.

The best indicator of your mental age is what fresh snow does to your sense of mobility.

Surprisingly, a holistic approach works only bottom-up, not top-down.

Regret is merely an internalized "I told you so".

Somewhere in a shed in China, someone is already making that brilliant product idea you just had. Unless you're Chinese yourself, of course.

If you want your innovative idea to succeed sooner, launch it in New Zealand.

"We need to go to more of these industry conferences & events" - a team on their way to becoming totally average in the industry.

Can someone remind me what the age cohort was that AB Males buy a pasta machine? I think it came just before the home bread baking machine age cohort.

There are few things more fun than disagreeing with people who know what they're talking about.

SO WHERE DOES THE FARAOH WANT HIS
PYRAMID? HE SUGGESTED WE START WITH
THIS POINTY BLOCK. QUICK, IT'S HEAVY.

Often the cure involves making you more ill first. Just like family photos emailed over from home make you more homesick rather than less.

The best dates to meet are the sweet ones that go into a baklava.

Whatever follows the word "objective" tends to be totally subjective.

Productive week huh? OK, but fighting global/regional teams, or any other group of colleagues doesn't count as productive. Think again.

Don't deal with shit by stepping on it.

Brave is the person who lets a promising idea prevail over short term profit. Hence the innovation always happens in the shed next door.

Beware, nutters can bring on an anaphylactic shock.

The best decisions are made based on a night's sleep, not an analyst's report.

Things besides politics you don't want to be fighting in your innovation project: gravity, floods, civil war, E-bola, migraine & nay-sayers.

I once worked with a brand team that were just like The Avengers. The only real difference was that they were all The Hulk.

BE SMART AND HIDE YOUR
PROCRASTINATION UNDER A SMILE
AND A THICK BLANKET OF QUESTIONS.

Successful innovation starts with actually doing what you were thinking.

Walking into a meeting you feel you cannot walk away from means, by definition, you've walked into a trap.

Unless you're in the business of building passenger aircraft, you really don't need 20 'critical success factors'. Probably 3 will do.

Of course the BRIC economies offer massive potential. Just don't forget the economies you conveniently share a border with.

If you're wondering how to make your "bad news" board presentation more enjoyable, inhale some helium - then pass the balloon around.

When typing a very big message on your very small phone - consider just making the phone-call instead. Your message will be much clearer.

When setting your team's KPIs, don't forget to specify along which axis you're stretching their goals.

A system is perfect only until the moment everyone understands it. From then on, everyone starts abusing it.

Virtual World corporations are complaining that patents are blocking innovation rather than driving it. Welcome to the Real World, children.

Most boutique services are at best canteen services, in clever disguise.

Be aware that email is a miscommunication accelerator.

After all these years, someone just told me of the Sunk Costs Fallacy. Well, I'm certainly not going to switch to using that non-sense now.

Hey solo professionals. Don't call yourself CEO of your company, it makes you look vain and rather silly.

Key to successful innovation is setting priorities and not being distrac

Alcohol and operating heavy machinery go together fine, but only in the right sequence.

If it takes your business 6 months to do something as simple as register a new vendor, how can you think you can launch a new product in 12?

The moment at which a piece of work is considered 'finished' depends more on the hour of the day than the finishing level of the work itself

A: "Hey, no need to be stressed about this"
B: "But what if it all goes wrong?"
A: "Then you won't have wasted your time stressing about it"."

Forever" equals about 5-6 months, in most business contexts.

"You need a clear ambition and a simple decision making process" - Great, just like Don Quixote.

> **In case of error – REWIND**
> **Crisis – FAST FORWARD**
> **Own stupidity – STOP**
> **Competitor's stupidity – RECORD**
> **Boredom – PLAY**

"I don't like their answer, so I'll ask a different question" - the logic behind many endless multi-disciplinary conversations.

The Entrepreneur's Dilemma: sustainable business growth implies/requires decreasing personal relevance. Ego's disguised as glass ceilings.

When working on your breakthrough innovation, don't forget the not-so-early adopters. They want a fun/tasty/useful product too.

> **Anticipation beats prediction.**

Successful negotiation is about keeping focus on what you agree on. Not what you disagree on.

A benefit of being able to change course quickly is that it allows you to be wrong quite often too.

Innovation in mature markets is almost always about getting consumers to switch away from something else.

You're probably your own bottleneck in many more ways than you realise.

Keep in mind most of your actions are in fact interactions.

Question: 3-year plans that need re-writing every year should really be named 1-year plans, right?

Your consumers WILL find out what you just did. Yes, you know what I mean.

"Action driven by fear of inaction", aka "Panic"

True innovation led by your R&D and Manufacturing teams flows not from more Process Control, but less: Process Liberation.

Do not underestimate the motivational power of a well-timed pat on the back.

From now on I will refer to "compromises" as "hybrid solutions".

A $1m incentive can bring down a $1bn empire. Decisions are made in the best interest of the decision maker, not the topic of decision.

"But won't this product cannibalise half our portfolio?" - "Yes, definitely. Or would you prefer a competitor to kill your cash cows?"

"Ambition" before "Exploration" before "Idea" before "Planning" before "Success". But only in the orderly world of the dictionary.

Lower ranks are applauded for bringing in fresh ideas. Higher ranks are applauded for not stopping them.

Corporate innovation paradox: regardless of the improbability of any idea making it to market, a ruthless emphasis on screening out ideas.

An excellent way to wean your customer off the old product onto the new model, is doing it abruptly, unannounced and without mercy.

Board room agreements are about business objectives, the fights are about the personal consequences.

On the long dark journey of getting innovations to market, even the doldrums have doldrums.

Moore's law for accelerating computing power must have a counterpart for humans dumbing down.

Multi-cultural/lingual corporate environments would do good to adopt the universal language of slapstick more often.

Of the nautical analogies used in business, the barnacle would deserve more attention. We all know one.

Don't forget to start work on V2 of your great new idea in parallel with the V1 launch. Because V2 is the one that just might make you money.

Option paralysis has little to do with the options and everything with the paralyzed.

Don't say your team won't follow up on your instructions until you've tried Kung Fu Briefing.

Things that speed up meetings and decision making: focused pre-reads, set agendas, action lists & full bladders.

In Foresight, It's All *So* Obvious.

**ISN'T IT GREAT YOU'LL SPEND
THE REST OF YOUR CAREER WORKING
ON THIS PRODUCT?**

This is about your bread & butter having become a commodity and you being on your way out of business. This is a bout Pricing having become the only tool you have left to influence your customer's decision making.

When you lose on price, you are in fact experiencing the consequence of something that happened much earlier and you're probably in even more trouble than you are aware of. What may appear like a stroke of bad luck could well be the sign of a deeper, more structural problem.

Imagine one of your customers has chosen to switch to a competitor's product, taking a significant chunk of your business away. A chat in the hallway of your company may then well sound like this:

A) Dude, why the long face? What's happening with that big [client] contract I heard you were bidding for?

B) Not good, it's over. I just heard we lost to [competitor]. A damn disgrace after 5 years of good business with [client].

A) What, you mean [competitor]? The amateurs who've been knocking off bad copies of our [product]?

B) Yes, the &*$)$@£ b**tards undercut our proposal by almost 40%. There was no way we could match that.

A) But their quality is appalling! I thought [client] was anal about quality?

B) They were, but not this time.

A) Surely that will get them in trouble, there's no way [competitor] can produce anything close to our standards. Our quality is FAR better, make that GALACTICALLY better than theirs.

B) I know, I know. Of course [client] will be back in six months, but that's still a lot of revenue gone. Not to mention my bonus.

A) Yeah, they'll be back. You just wait 'till they've really experienced the importance of quality when it comes to [product].

Feel free to insert you own favourites for [client], [competitor] and [product]. What has gone so wrong for these poor people? What to do now? Well, depending on who you are (or whom you ask), you may be considering one of the following:

- You're confident [client] will come back soon, so you'll just lower capacity for 6 months, fire some folks and wait.

- You consider manufacturing more efficiently, invest more in Six Sigma, Lean and DFE to get that cost down.

- You'd rather lower your margin to keep the business, it'll never be good enough for the shareholders anyway, so screw 'em.

- You consider lowering your quality standards and simplify your manufacturing process.

- You now have time to improve quality even further, making [client] return sooner.

- You spend the next twelve months planning a hostile takeover of [competitor].

- You put your R&D at work to develop [product]-LIGHT, the cheap alternative.

- You'll take [competitor] to court for infringing copyrights or patents.

There are many more things you could do, the problem is none of them will do you much good unless you start repairing some of the damage done way before you lost this contract. So here's another way of looking at the situation, which highlights your real problem.

Imagine you are now [competitor] and you're celebrating your first win over the industry leader. You proudly stroll through your rickety old factory where you've been knocking off countless copies for years, shaking hands as you go around. What are you going to do with this new revenue stream you've just secured?

- Buy a Ferrari, build an extension to your condo and finally take that holiday to the Bahamas.

- Invest in new machinery and get rid of the old crap you used to call assets.

- Put a quality control system in place, because you know [client] can be a little anal.

- Hire a colleague for your lonely engineer and get them to work on [product] v2.0.

- Hire a production manager, poach a marketer and assign a sales director, to free up your time for chasing more [client]s.

Obviously everyone should do something fun and silly like that first point, but as long as they back it up by one or more of the others they can only win. They simply re-invest. They are on the first step of a tricky but rewarding road past the original industry leader(s). They already know how do produce efficiently, they're not burdened by the hassle of developing from scratch and they operate in a mature market well developed by the leaders. According to Blue Ocean Strategy [Kim & Mauborgne] that was a bad place to be... well, that's not so true if you're the underdog.

So where does that leave the current industry leaders? Is there no hope? Up in the ivory tower of quality premium goods, looking down onto the bogs of low-cost copy-cats, they can become overly concerned about keeping the tower intact. That is indeed hopeless. The trick is to realize how to modify the tower and do so in time.

Most businesses understand they need to change the tower by evolving it a little to adapt to changing customer & consumer needs. Maybe stretch the brand a little and try attracting a new target group. There are a bazillion books out there explaining how to do that, if you aren't doing that already.

True long term success comes from exploiting your ivory tower's high-altitude panoramic view – and look for crumbling towers in other categories. New markets where your proposition would in fact be the underdog, but one that can provide a smart solution to conundrums your Heimat market has already dealt with. Mature markets with a flaw they weren't aware of, yet. Most often the flaw is a poor price/quality ratio, which is exactly what [competitor] is doing to your business right now. Become a game changer. These oceans are Blue, but not *empty* and entering these will almost always involve tearing down competing towers.

In the end it's quite simple ...

When others start moving IN

... you need to move ON

... or they will catch up with you.

In hindsight, every success seems like the result of strategic brilliance.

Once launched, breakthrough innovation has only two possible endpoints:
1) mainstream
2) vintage futurology books

Emotions are irrelevant, right up to the moment they hit you.

Maybe change programs by definition have only a start and no end point. In the end, it's a choice to no longer stand still.

Then again, change for change's sake is mere restlessness.

Banks not providing credit to small businesses will lead to a new generation of healthier businesses that doesn't need banks. Darwin lives on.

Innovation becoming mainstream means that at any given point in time, someone, somewhere, is working on the next inflatable umbrella.

Not so long ago, "working hard" and "long hours" were seen as a lack of success. What IDIOT spun that round?

Of course the main reason the Z-Generation is so agile in today's tech world is their fingers are still small enough to operate modern phones

Why are there no futurologists and/or trend agencies in the Fortune500? There should be if they were any good.

Breakthrough only counts after having broken through.

"Less is More" tends to be just less.

Stay true to your roots, your principles & in twenty years people will finally understand what you really are: a stubborn, old fashioned git.

Funny how you need friends, an accountant & cash to set up a small business, but only friends & an accountant to take over a $10Bn empire.

A brand's product portfolio is only as weak as its strongest link.

Keep a close eye on your competition and be guaranteed to overlook the company that will put you AND the competition out of business.

"Best in category" solutions/people/companies were first "not in category". Not "mediocre in category".

Great innovations never perish without worthy successors. Sorry, make that: even great innovations are eventually trumped by better ones.

Try writing a paragraph of text on innovation without using the letter 'i'. And then you notice a second reason that's difficult.

The fast track to success for your big idea is enabling everyone to take credit for it. Just swallow your ego and try to smiling while it happens.

Treat every idea with the certainty there will be another, better one.

The Next Big Thing is very difficult to spot early, simply because it's often disguised as The Current Small Thing.

Wouldn't it be great if your last failure was all due to bad luck and your current success is all thanks to your unique style and talent?

When gathering confidence for doing new things... Remember to stop doing some old things.

The benchmark for new ideas is not what came before, but what comes after.

There's no stopping an idea whose time has gone.

Superimposing Henry Ford onto Steve Jobs: "if I'd asked The People what they wanted, they'd have asked for nothing more than a bigger iPod".

Try imagining Steve McQueen racing the streets of Bullitt's San Francisco in a Toyota Prius - innovation suddenly loses some of its shine.

If you suspect a competitor is evolving the category at the fringes, they've probably already revolutionized the core without you noticing.

For every great idea you put your money on, there are at least ten better ones. But don't worry, you'll find that out in hindsight.

Given the low number of historically proven perfect solutions, the one you just came up with will probably be trumped too. Hope it's by you.

For ideas to get noticed on a horizon far away, they'll need to be big. Unless there's a trail of smaller ones leading there.

Put together, a historian and a futurologist know exactly nothing about the present. But the debate will be massively opinionated.

The pixelated, low resolution world of Legoland proves that High Definition is not necessarily the only way forward.

Just when you thought you were finished, your competition shows you you're not even close. And they're thinking the same.

Perfection would be a great goal to pursue, if it weren't for normality improving so fast.

Perfection is grossly overrated as an endpoint in development.

When you (person/business) think you're finally getting good at something, you are in fact starting to flatline at the top of your S-curve.

Great inventions often happen simultaneously in different categories, cultures & continents. New TV formats show it's true for bad ones too.

Candid Camera: try explaining to anyone under 30 why it was either funny or remarkable. They'll probably post your attempt on YouTube.

What does an ideal, perfectly optimized business process look like? From the comfort of your bed, charging money for stuff you're not doing.

Soon, the world will rebel against baristas insisting on placing a lid on your cappuccino before you reach the condiment counter.

Your comfort zone should lie behind you.

Miracles and Puzzles describe exactly the same reality, yet the former elicits passive submission and the latter active curiosity.

In a cab in Toronto... Driving down Avenue Road... Amazed about city planners' lack of inspiration in naming this street.

The problem when "doing nothing" turns out to be the best option is that no one wants to take credit for it.

I love my paper books. They smell nicer than eBooks and I'm pretty confident they'll also outlive the *.opf and *.azw file formats.

How do you explain the concept of a joystick to a Y-Gen without sounding A) old-fashioned B) perverted?

The only way to beat a competitor with a longer term view than yours is bankruptcy. As for them, it's just another battle.

I think people retiring at 40, 55 or 70 have all spent roughly the same number of hours working. Only those retiring at 30 found a shortcut.

Mobile phones, laptops, work/private life blurring... All mainstream now. Maybe City bankers really are the Avant Garde of trend setters.

Motels. Now there's a category in dire need of some positive reframing.

Just like in Scooby Doo, competition monsters always turn out to be just a person in a suit.

SIR, THIS IS A SOCIAL MEDIA START-UP. THE BUSINESS MODEL IS THAT YOU GIVE ME MONEY.

You won't believe how small your old comfort zone looks when you return to it a few years later.

First-time-right breakthrough innovation lives in business books, MBA courses, board rooms and at the end of the rainbow.

The difference between what is 'real' and what is 'authentic' is not what they are but what's driving them.

In retrospect, people will claim to already have heard of your successful idea about a year before you had it.

I hear tuition fees at the University Of Life are now even higher than those at The School Of Hard Knocks.

Revolutionary new products and services, just like any other revolutionaries, destroy as much as they create. Without exception, nor mercy.

Innovation to romantics is complex and mysterious beauty, to rationalists complex yet cerebral fun - meanwhile the empiricists just go do it.

If you implement creativity like a religion, you'll need miracles to be successful.

Differentiating innovation is about transcending category barriers and leaving them for the competition to trip over.

When Y-Gens talk about family babies, they always refer to nephews and nieces. I think Y-Gens will be extinct soon.

Life never gives lemons to people with a citrus juicer close by.

I hope the day caffeine is revealed as lethal, is after it's ended my life enjoying it.

It's sad when great products are phased out without a proper successor - Concorde, Space Shuttle, Customer Service, Gasoline, Journalism.

Thank god your competitor's innovation projects are not leading anywhere either. It's probably a non-competitor who'll ruin you both.

When things start falling apart, it seems like 'dignity' is either the first or the last to go.

The Innovator's Hell: a burning, flaming oven full of happy, fully satisfied consumers.

First Diet, then Health, then Wellness, then Vitality... How many trends are left to go before Perpetual Nirvana?

Why were so few heritage brands created after the 70's? Well, ask any of today's brand managers "Hey, want this job for the next 15 years?"

Plotting strategy only on strengths (and no vision) is like telling a marathon runner to go run as far as possible, without telling where to.

Somewhere out there, someone is making a living out of doing the exact opposite of what you are doing.

What ever happened to the company that made all the beige pigment used in desktop computers? I hope they're OK.

With the number of caesarean births rising fast, there is nothing stopping us humans evolving brains the size of watermelons.

The Entrepreneur Trap: with no one telling you what to do, you're never ever finished.

Innovations that create new jobs also destroy old ones, by definition.

$$[\text{(proof you're wrong) / (proof you're right)} = \text{(PR expenses)}]$$

"Welcome back" and "Welcome home" are a world apart.

Brand innovation tends to be driven by a single person's urge to leave a mark - and then any mark will do.

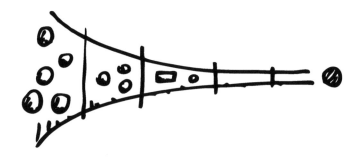

Ceci n'est pas une pipe-ligne d'innovation.

You know you're too old to be a 'high potential' once you realize you're hiring them.

Whatever nearly kills you, doesn't make you stronger. Having nearly killed you, it probably badly damaged and weakened you.

In business, you always have two options: the wrong one, and the uncertain one.

Is it me, or do troubled professionals who visit career coaches have an above average tendency to become career coaches?

From down here on the ground, people with a helicopter view are just noisy specks.

A holistic approach means vertically through the organizational layers, as much as horizontally across disciplines.

I have a hunch that market cycles influence innovation far less than career cycles do.

Yes, I understand you have a vision and dedication. But what you need is an objective and a budget.

Sadly, few things are true 'only because you say so'. Simply not good enough a reason. Except when raising children.

Being underestimated works well on the long term. And vice versa for the exact opposite.

Planning for success is too often forgotten.

Companies succeed even when choosing wrongly, often because competition doesn't choose at all.

Focusing on the competition means that by definition you do not have the initiative.

To anyone complaining how the current string of crises is haltering the upward flow of civilization... our history IS a string of crises.

For some reason, in today's app developing start-ups it is considered a good sign if the company founders are running for the exit. #Bubble

Less is Less, unless you offer More. #Simple

Those little coffee brewers in hotel rooms should be labelled "ONLY IN CASE OF EMERGENCY", just to manage expectations.

The smörgåsbord of life usually presents itself like an IKEA canteen.

Eating insects gross? Most people don't like recognizing their meat either. Can't we just grind up grasshoppers and mould them into burgers?

Key to a healthy lifestyle: everything in moderation. Including moderation.

Small businesses dream of being big and strong, whilst the big ones wish they were smaller and more agile. Don't we all?

Wrong place at the wrong time? Errr. No, I'd say wrong ingredients at the wrong temperature.

Perfect, Free, Instant and Self-Sustaining - the unbeatable proposition. Just so you know how competition will put you out of business.

I often find "walking away" much more courageous than "sticking with it".

"The world just won't understand the brilliance of my idea" - Stubbornness is a two-way street.

Shopping abroad, we all have small change angst.

Advertising via social media. Imagine your $2m billboard campaign being 'unfriended' with a click of a button.

Let's not be too dramatic about wishing time travel were possible into the distant past. One minute is probably enough for even the stickiest situations.

The Cost-Value Wormhole. When you save so much cost from your A-brand product that it emerges as inferior to the B-brand alternative.

If the time isn't right for your new idea, then find another place, not another time.

Unsolved puzzles of modern Man: squaring the circle - JFK's assassination - superconductivity at room temperature - hotel shower controls.

No matter how advanced our technology becomes, humanity will always remain a sucker for coupons.

If you can get away with ordering less than one Venti™ Cappuccino an hour, it's cheaper to live in a Starbucks than in a London City condo.

Of the biggest benefit of staying in a hotel in your home country is that none of the TV channels seem even remotely odd.

Another day, another flight, another 100kgs CO2. Really worried that I'll wake up one morning with a Greenpeace activist chained to my leg.

The fact you don't hear of many successful introverts just shows you don't know who's really running the world around you.

Do NOT eat beef noodles in front of your laptop.

Returning to your old comfort zone is like returning to your home village. Cosy, but everything seems so small & a little old fashioned.

Einstein's theory of relativity and time elasticity can be experienced personally by experimenting with travel with- or without children.

Maybe bio-gas would be more successful if it smelled nicer?

Too many architects forget their designs need to withstand weather and soil - after ten years they look worse than tattoos twice their age.

When pampered people mistake their skewed interpretation of Maslow's Pyramid for being the societal norm, embarrassing things happen.

Assuming perpetually rising productivity, every innovation destroys more jobs than it creates, by definition. #KillerLogic

Don't forget to feed your cash cows or the moving average of private label mediocrity WILL catch up with them.

I have a hunch that success is mostly about managing luck – and then resisting the temptation to gamble.

The closest exit may be behind you #metaphors

It's not about being advanced and innovative. It's about looking incredibly normal and making everything else look hopelessly outdated.

Contrary to Newtonian physics, the centrifugal force in spinning businesses sends the lighter bodies flying out instead of the heavier ones.

If you don't arm your troops with decision making capabilities and simple values, requests become commands, susceptible to noise on the line

Filters get clogged and become bottlenecks. That is not just an analogy, it is what actually happens with all filters around you.

What do you call the bit that's left after you sold all the valuable parts of a business?

Is it a platform-quality idea? Well, what do you think are the chances it will outlive you and make your adult grandchildren smile?

Two-way broadcasting is not a conversation.

Most foresight projects end up becoming insight projects because of how long it takes them to get signed off and started.

"You know what you should do? You should stress less." - the ultimate in useless advice.

UGH.
SOMEONE WITH HELICOPTER VIEW.

"Customer Success Manager" - that puts the pressure entirely on the wrong person in the equation, no?

Whoever coined the phrase "Talk is cheap" clearly wasn't using a Swiss mobile phone provider.

"Hey, that's an interesting observation! Let's pigeonhole it" - everyone in Western society, since Aristotle.

"Oh you meant a LAUNCH date! I thought you just wanted to get together for a bite to eat." - When executive lunch dates get awkward.

"I'll make him an offer he can't reuse" - Marketing, in a nutshell.

"I didn't buy X for $Y, so I actually earned $Y and can now spend $(Y-10%) on Z and still save money" - Banks, EU-budgets and Girlie Logic.

Complaining implies you're putting control of the solution in someone else's hands. Not a good idea.

Not all market launches cost tons of money. Some also cost you your marriage, health and sanity.

Power is about access, not money.

"Our CEO instructed our team to be more entrepreneurial" - oxymoron

In the grand scheme of things, it's the small schemes that make all the difference.

"Taking life not too seriously" - FYI this means taking life very seriously. And everything else a lot less.

Now that corporate giants are financially healthier and larger than most countries, I wonder how long before they hand out citizenships?

The main reason there is so little entrepreneurialism in big corporate environments is that no one is confident spelling it.

I AGREE IT'S NOT A VERY LONG TERM OUTLOOK, BUT IT'S WITHIN OUR RESEARCH TEAM'S STATISTICAL CONFIDENCE REQUIREMENTS.

In the canteen of life, we're all handed a wet tray.

"Micro-management" only appears as such when you're on the receiving end.

What makes you tired by day, keeps you awake at night.

Inventions we're eagerly waiting for are promised by the experts "within the next 5 years". Yet we never expected the ones we use every day.

The more complex your strategy, the easier it'll be to post-rationalise all credit towards you, or the blame away from you.

There is only ONE real reason new product launches fail. And the other reason is lack of focus.

In the controlled chaos of doing business, we all get dirty. It's just a question whether it gathers on you or in you.

I tell myself my endless running with luggage & catching flights is today's version of paleolithic me chasing wild boar and hauling it home.

Eager for breakthrough innovation? Ask not how to revolutionise YOUR category, ask how your capabilities can revolutionise ANOTHER category.

"When projects go into the blame-storming phase, too often fingers are pointed at the Boogie" - the Jacksons

Is there a scientific term for panicking over what might happen in case of a panic?

On sports analogies in business: I think they clay tennis court sweeper and the equestrian obstacle hedge trimmer deserve more reference.

Are things really getting better or have you merely revised your expectations?

"Let's get our twenty brightest minds together and refine this idea to perfection" – famous last words.

Second
thoughts from a
GRUMPY
innovator

written & illustrated by costas papaikonomou

> **The future isn't in front of you, but
> *behind* you. Merciless in pursuit, on
> your heels, preying on every last decision
> you made, awaiting your next move.**

Second Thoughts

In 2012, I published the first Grumpy Innovator book about the ugly reality of innovation in corporate environments and the responses have been heart-warming;

- "Thank god I am not alone, I thought I was the crazy one here at the office."

- "I read a few lines every time I'm in the toilet. I've found it a great inspiration and laxative."

- "It made me laugh and then cry when I realised I was the topic of the joke myself."

- "It made me cry in the toilet at the office, thank god I was alone at the time."

Three years later, there is good news and bad news.

The good news is that the book has put me in touch with countless new friends, who share my amazement of how organisations deal with innovation and get in trouble when they need to do doing things differently in order to grow, or even survive. There is an army of us out there, who will patiently sit through long meetings and tedious processes, waiting for the right moment to do what we know is required to actually get things done.

The bad news is we're still a minority and I'm still grumpy. Which is why you're now holding this second book: I've had no problem finding more stuff to write about.

Scattered across these pages you will find further thoughts on reasons why innovation is still a painful activity for so many businesses.

Premise: why I'm still grumpy

In the first Grumpy Innovator book I explored the paradox of innovation[2]. The conflict between a messy, ever-changing outside world which drives the need to innovate, versus wanting a predictable, calm environment in which it is easier to run a profitable business. In corporate ecosystems, this leads to over-relying on models and abstract views of the world, resulting in poor success rates. It was also fun to throw rocks at various functions who we all know get in the way of things more than anything.

What I'd like to explore with you in this second book is a number of perspectives on 'innovation' itself. What is it, how does it strain people & processes and what core competencies does a business need to do it well? But most of all to throw a couple more rocks and have some fun.

On the next two pages is a diagram showing the Sunny Smile of Innovation alongside its dark mirror image, the Murky Mechanics of Innovation. We'll explore how innovation is more than the business textbook definition of 'doing something new that makes money' or 'drives growth'. It comes in different shades and cannot be seen without its implications on the organisation delivering it.

---

[2] You can find the first book's premise on page 146

Sunny Smile Of Innovation

Innovation is a commercial tool for businesses to
continuously seek out new revenue opportunities, and

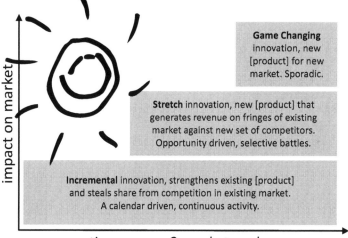

Game Changing innovation, new [product] for new market. Sporadic.

Stretch innovation, new [product] that generates revenue on fringes of existing market against new set of competitors. Opportunity driven, selective battles.

Incremental innovation, strengthens existing [product] and steals share from competition in existing market. A calendar driven, continuous activity.

impact on market

time passes & market evolves

that's the bright happy side shown here.

- **Incremental**: this is your 'new news' process. Small
  tweaks to satisfy new questions from existing
  users/clients and piss off competition.
- **Stretch**: find new occasions and formats to draw in an
  audience just beyond your current reach. Great if you're
  starting to lose on price in your current market and
  things are commoditizing.
- **Game Changers**: The sexy end of the spectrum, where
  you create a lasting legacy, get your face on magazine
  covers and re-invent the industry.

Murky Mechanics Of Innovation

When most business books and creative gurus talk about 'disruption', they refer to messing up your competitors' heads and shaking up the market.

impact on organisation

Incremental, change settings in the factory & update sales team. **6-18 Months.**

Stretch, find gap with new target audience, get R&D to develop new [product], order new lines in factory, train sales team and build relationships with new buyers. **A year or two?**

Game Changing, as Stretch *plus* develop new technical capabilities & IP, create new business model, build new factory, find new suppliers, replace personnel by new team with right skill set, create new distribution, ditch existing portfolio & its revenue stream. **OMFG Kill Me.**

time & resource requirements

That's *not* it. You are disrupting yourself much more.

- **Incremental**: a cross-functional effort you can tightly plan and control, within set ecosystems.
- **Stretch**: Requires understanding new category consumers and business rules, creation of minor new capability and your best bet for growing your market when you're still calling the shots.
- **Game Changers**: Only when your back is against the wall, your current [product] is completely commoditized or the market is going extinct.

So what does this dark and disheartening mirror image mean? It shows that not only do you need particular functions inside your business to innovate pragmatically in a messy world to keep the machines running[3], you also need an additional set of meta-capabilities to adapt your organisation as much as the market you're serving;

- The ability to share responsibility for innovation across functions; in parallel, not sequentially, with the lead switching sensibly as the work progresses. Similarly, realising that the source of the opportunity can come from anywhere too – sales, technology, distribution, etcetera – *not* just consumer focus groups and market research.
- Acute awareness of the required impact your innovation needs to make in order to achieve your business objective. Create an incremental innovation when that'll do the job, reserve game changers for when you need (or can afford) one.
- Savvy use of expensive assets over time, retaining function and relevance beyond the initially intended launch products and support future revenue as well.
- Install processes across the business functions that drive for value-add to the end result, your product. Not solely to optimize operational efficiency. It is the simplest way to ensure you keep aiming for relevancy *and* pick up early signals of change right at the source: the customers of your products and services.
- Acknowledgment that when you move up into Stretch and Game Changing innovation, you are also moving *away* from daily procedures and into new ball games with unknown rules. That means success will depend more than anything on the judgment of the people

---

[3] See first Grumpy Innovator book

creating the innovation, not on prescribed ways of working. *Trust* them.

I'll share my grumpy thoughts on pitfalls on these five principles, along with ways that might make life just a little easier. Might. A little.

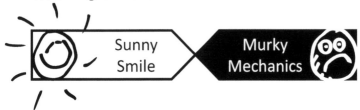

You may now be thinking... wait a moment, aren't today's celebrated new heroes of innovation in the digital arena doing all that Game Changing in the blink of an eye *and* making a fortune on the go?

Yes – *and*.

Putting those new digital heroes in a more realistic and perhaps even cynical perspective;

- The vast majority of the global economy runs on businesses who *make* things, not on digital platforms for selling or accessing them. This will remain the case in our lifetime, at least as long as humans consume physical foods & goods.
- Most, if not *all* billion-dollar start-ups prove to be pyramid schemes, not making any profitable revenue stream, ever. Then they collapse.
- The digital space is big and sexy, but it's also an immature Wild West in comparison to say, laundry detergents, chewing gum or dry soups.

This book is for people who are in the business of making and selling real things, to highly competitive mass markets around the globe. People building brands by carefully crafting relevant improvements to win their consumers' hearts. For them, the Murky Mechanics Of Innovation are a reality that tires them by day and keeps them awake at night.

I salute you.

Costas Papaikonomou
June 2015

Which mouths do I put my money in?

**THE FINANCE TEAM IS PRETTY SURE
THIS IS WHAT OUR CONSUMERS WANT.**

Which mouths do I put my money in?

Somewhere, early autumn: a cross-functional discussion in a corporate meeting room.

CEO: *Knocks on table with toy hammer.*
"My dearest Innovation Committee, that was a good start. Now let's move on to agenda item 2. By the way, who's taking notes today? Anyway – ahem – agenda item 2 is to allocate our innovation budgets for the next 5 years. I have 10 million cash-thingies reserved. What do you think?"

R&D: "Well, that depends. It's ₵3m more than we had last year before you came on board. Which is great, as we overspent ₵2m this year on catching up with [competitor]. But it was worth it as we are now ready to file patents of our own and won't need to work with [supplier] anymore."

Finance: "Did you budget for filing patents? That's expensive."

R&D: *Ruffles papers.*
"Well, that depends. We did for US & Europe, but Sales wants to ship [product] to Asia."

Finance: "So that's a No."
Scribbles in notepad, with stern face.

Marketing: "Sorry I'm late. What are we discussing today?"

CEO: "Innovation budgets for the next 5 years. And late arrivals get note-taking duty. We just started and R&D is asking for ₵2m to plug last year's gap."

Marketing: "We need to change that notes rule, it's unfair to busy people. But good to hear we're talking innovation. I need a game changer next year. After that I don't know yet. How much does a game changer cost?"

R&D: "Well, that depends. Do you have a spec?"

Marketing: "No, I'm waiting for the U&A to come in."

Market Research: "Preliminary U&A findings are due in 3 months."

Marketing: "Hey, I hadn't seen you were here. Hi. But wait, you said 3 months at last month's meeting too."

Market Research: "Yes, and then you all-of-a-sudden urgently wanted to include Asia, while fieldwork in Europe and North America had already started. And don't look at me like that."
Rolls eyes.

Marketing: "Ya Ya. Touché. Anyway, without a spec, how much does a game changer cost? Ball-park will do."

R&D: "Well, that depends. Last year's [game changer] was only ¢5m but it did take 4 years to develop. Do you want to know what we can do in 1 year or do you want a game changer?"

Marketing: "I'm not sure I understand but either way, I can't spec without the U&A and I do need something next year."

Manufacturing: *Raises finger.*
"Sorry, can I say something?"

Marketing: "Maybe you can work from the segmentation? The infographics are really inspiring and it's pretty accurate except for France."

Sales: "Hey hold on, France just happens to be the only market that consistently makes the numbers. Remember who's paying the salaries here. We are."

CEO: "Guys, just a second. Manufacturing would like to say something."

Manufacturing: "Thank you. Well, I just wanted to say 3 of our 4 plants are severely underutilized already, since the orders for the last [game changer] have been disappointing. If we scrap all that kit now, we won't hit the ROI we promised."

CEO: "OK, that's a clear message. I suggest we forget about the game changers for next year and ensure we utilize our factories a bit better first. We have shareholder value to protect. The Six Sigma team are on the case, no?"

Manufacturing: "Plants. They're called plants, not factories. And the Six Sigma guys have indeed optimized the lines such we can make [game changer] more effectively, but we haven't anything new to fill the excess capacity so we're now nearing 30% idle."

CEO: "Sorry, plants. Not factories. Whatever. But are you saying TQM has made our plants more effective or less effective? I'm confused now."

Sales: "Hey hold on. You're changing the subject. How do I beat off [competitor product] if I can barely offer parity with [our product], even when I cut out all the margin? What do we do about that first?"

R&D: "Well, that depends. We could go back in time, properly spec it and then design it cheaper, faster and better. Shall we do that? Oh no – DUH – time travel hasn't been invented yet."

Marketing: "Ya Ya. Spare me the sarcasm. Our whole marketing team was different 2 years ago, how could *they* know what *we* would want to work on, eh? Besides, I want a game changer because I have a brand to build.
I'll cut the comms budget to fund new kit in the factory if I need to."

Finance: "You'll do what? Cash-thingies cannot be moved around like that. Comms, factories, we need to follow the process, ISO audit season is coming."

Manufacturing: "They're called *plants*, please. And that's exactly how we funded the new lines 4, 6, 11 and 14 years ago. I know because I was there every time to sign the paperwork."

CEO: *Knocks toy hammer on table again.*
"This is going nowhere. I asked a simple question at the beginning. How do we spend our ₵10m over the next 5 years? We need to innovate because that's what well run businesses do. Fewer Bigger Better.
Who owns the Innovation Funnel? I mean the Stage Gate"

All: "Market Research!" "Marketing!"

CEO: "What?"

Manufacturing: "Well, Supply Chain write all the contracts for anything new we do. But they're not part of this Innovation Committee. They're the only people *we* deal with when sorting out capacity, suppliers or anything new and that's been working fine for twenty years."

Market Research: "Ha! Well, we're a consumer centric company now and they don't represent our consumer. That time is behind us. Market Research should own the innovation funnel because *we* are the Voice Of The Consumer."

R&D "You mean you put every single one of my team's ideas in front of your focus groups. That's where most of my overspend went."

CEO: *Hammers more loudly now.*
"Jeez, settle down guys. Last time I checked, Procurement is part of Supply Chain and since we initiated the PartnersPlus programme, they control what market research we buy too. Now, can someone make a note to invite Supply Chain at next month's meeting to present the Innovation Funnel or Stage Gate or whatever it is they do to chart how we spend innovation budgets around here?
Now, who's making notes?"

Hopefully, you recognize nothing whatsoever of that scene and you have the innovation responsibilities clearly defined in your organization. Then the problem of budgeting for the future becomes as simple as: how much do I spend on what and when?

The problem with innovation resource is of course it's about planning for unknown solutions to yet uncertain problems and the further out in time you look the worse it gets. The only thing certain is it will be expensive, and there's never enough cash. The business books talk about building a car while driving it, but none mention the blinking fuel indicator.

Then how place your bets, when it comes to innovation investments? Is it about bringing the trend watchers in and watching them perform their 2×2 magic on flipcharts? Is it about sinking money in local start-ups hoping for a return? Or simply spend it on 10% free-wheeling time for your technical teams?

The problem of course, is the immensely different time lines that your technical and marketing teams operate on. Ask your R&D team how long it takes to develop a particular capability and the default answer is 5 years, plus a request for an expensive piece of laboratory kit. Ask your marketing team what new products they expect to need in 5 years' time and they'll tell you what they think they might need next year, along with a massive market research budget.

In essence, both teams are right. In the myopic world of foresight, they're saying the same thing: "We don't know how the future will affect us". Which is useless if you need to decide now where to invest for long term capabilities, be it technical or operational.

The answer lies in de-constructing this huge question into smaller chunks *and* the simple ambition to shape the future instead of just trying to guess what might happen. Remarkable opportunities reveal themselves when you look at the future through different lenses for things you can do;

- **Consumer & society**. What's going on in the lives of your end-consumer, throughout the day? How do the different generations use your products and what does that say about their next life stage?
- **Technology**. What are barriers you and your competitors are all running into, the contradictions and trade-offs that come with delivering your core benefit?
- **Channel & distribution**. How are the channels you are in now evolving? How do you make those even easier for your products to run through? What new channels are emerging?
- **Point of sale**. Will your end-users be buying products from you at the same point in time and place, or is this likely to change? Same for your middleman or retailer.
- **Environment & supply chain**. How can environmental impact be reduced, not just for ethical reasons, but also to overcome rising scarcity of just about every raw ingredient known to man?
- **Legal**. What does the regulatory landscape look like, what new rules and limitations are likely to be imposed on you? Look at categories that might serve as ominous precedents.
- **Brand**. If you were to just extrapolate what your brands have been doing so far, what would the effect be of multiplying by ten times faster, softer, harder, smoother, nicer …?

Etcetera. Defining the right set of lenses is *not* an exact science[4], the trick is to cast a wide net of relevant yet distinctly different directions that matter for your business.

Explore future scenarios first, through each of your lenses. Go further out than you'd ever be comfortable with for ROI calculations, it's OK. Have your technical and commercial teams spend some quality time together on thinking up what *the world* will look like in 5 to 10 years' time, not what they will be doing themselves. How will these changes affect your industry, your category, your markets. Ideate for 15-20 product/service concepts that would do well in your future world.

>>> PAUSE FOR SIDE STEP:

If you're struggling to go beyond the obvious, use this simple old Soviet[5] trick. In the future, everything becomes more ideal at delivering its core benefit:

1. **Perfectly,** at optimal impact, sweetness, delight and efficacy.
2. **Instantly,** only when and where necessary.
3. **Autonomously,** with no material nor info required from the beneficiary.
4. **Free** to the recipient.

Just think about it - if any competitor would introduce something that surpasses you on one of those four dimensions, you're in trouble. If they hit 2 or more - you're **toast** - and you don't need a single focus group nor technology scan to figure that out. But you will need to be clear on

---

[4] *In fact, people stating that looking into the future is a science with any degree of certainty, have no more accuracy than a horoscope. Anyone with actual certainty about the future would not be telling nor selling it to you, but using that information to make bazillions in the stock market.*
There are no trend agencies in the Fortune500 last time I checked.

[5] *TRIZ — go check Wikipedia. It's the closest you'll get to objective problem solving.*

```
what your core benefit actually is as it might
not be what you think. For example, if you're in
the business of lawnmowers: the ideal isn't an
autonomous robo-mower, nor ceramic blades, nor
solar power. Because the core benefit that people
want is nice lawns, the ideal result is more
likely to be self-cutting grass. Which means your
future might lie crop genetics which is a
completely different industry from garden
machinery.

Shaping the Future implies tackling category
barriers.

<<< END OF SIDE STEP.
```

Chart & rank what technical capabilities you'd need to create your concepts for a future world. For every one of your future concepts, list a maximum of 3 new capabilities you would need to have matured in order to deliver them profitably. Again, go 360: review technology, supply chain, sourcing, distribution and so on. Not the functional teams in your business, but the capabilities you'd need to develop if you were a start-up. Chart the overlap between them across concepts. Which capabilities appear over and over, as critical for multiple concepts? You're getting warmer now, most likely a top-5 of core capabilities is emerging: the platforms that will give you most bang for buck wherever the future winners turn out to be.

Review their implications, and then some more. This is where it gets fun. For each of the key capabilities, list the implications across your business (internal) and market (external) of implementing them. Then list the implications of those implications. You'll be surprised at what that second round reveals. Most likely, your list of core capabilities halved along the way, and at least one new joiner appeared.

Ask yourself what you need just to play the game and where you can excel to win? This automatically takes you into 'make or buy' considerations. This last step is surprisingly easy and shamefully often overlooked. Practice saying "MAKE or BUY?" out loud in front of a mirror, and then in front of your technical team, it will turn heads. For some reason, too many organizations culturally assume everything needs to be developed from scratch. Look again at your shortlist of capabilities you need in order to thrive in the future, in the context of what passed in all three steps before. Which of them are actually mere nice-to-haves, platform standards that most likely already exist in other industries? Just BUY them, now. Then ask yourself what are the ownable, differentiating capabilities you want to excel at and win? MAKE them or buy the companies that make them. Start developing and patenting like there is no tomorrow. Because there is.

Are you awaiting the future, or shaping it?

Charting innovation bets and deciding where to invest your innovation budget becomes much easier once you realize you don't need 20-20 vision on what the future will bring, nor spreading the bet across a huge number of alternatives. As long as you know what you need to be good at.

> **Innovation success is mostly about luck, and resisting the temptation to gamble**.

"Stop being so stressed" - the single most useless advice you can receive when you're stressed.

Most Marketers talk with their Manufacturing team just like they talk to the guy in the blue overall who repairs their car. Fearful & impatient.

If you're considering developing complicated products for Millennials, be aware that by the time you launch they'll be nearing 40.

Everything so far in your career is a consequence of your own choices. So is everything from here on.

Innovative destruction and hopelessness: long queues for collecting benefits. By that I mean marketers lining up for focus groups.

"I had a beer, please"
A futurologist walks into a bar

Hey Marketer, if you want your CEO to suck up every opinion you ventilate, pre-empt it by "we've been hearing in focus groups that..."

Consumer centricity =
[time spent convincing consumers] /
[time spent convincing internal stakeholders].
Try scoring > 1%

Love as marketing concept statement:
You're lonely & need love
Discover Me
You'll feel super amazing
Because only I give TLC
Me Me Me

Success in market is less dependent on the perfect idea, than it being an idea a small team is willing to work overtime for to improve and make a reality.

Time for my legal team meeting to discuss our new claims strategy!
Packs wooden stakes, crucifixes and garlic.

"We will do focus groups to let our consumers define our strategy", he said, followed by the hissing sound of all hope deflating into a vacuum.

"Fewer & Bigger Innovation" also implies "Less Innovations". Which means the required competence isn't scaling but the ability to choose.

To pessimists, the glass is half empty.
Meanwhile, the optimists are making a mess and splashing water all over themselves.

**COVERING YOUR ARSE IN PILES OF RESEARCH
JUST MAKES IT LOOK BIGGER.**

A management culture of looking down the hierarchy for answers ("you tell me what to choose") is passed down all the way to the focus group.

"We have an informal, flat organisation", said the Secretary General.

Millennials, temper your heroic expectations.
Actual things you do before you die: sore joints, dementia, kidney stones & maybe cough blood.

A framework for "judging quality" isn't meant for "creating quality", ie. reviewers are not the makers. In business that is misunderstood.

Navigating your innovation project through murky C-Suite waters will likely involve more coochy-coochy with your CFO than your CEO or CMO.

"I can change him!"
***Women attracted to the wrong men
and marketers trying to attract consumers.***

Nature's fundamental Weak, Strong, Electro-Magnetic and Gravity forces ... meet their corporate mirror Wimp, Ego, Internet and Guru forces.

Bulls and China shops. Sometimes it really is the China shop's fault.

Hey Boomers, the house with the big mortgage you're leaving as inheritance would be better named as 'tax bill', 'debt' or just 'no house'.

Buying stock of a business that's never made profit: gambling. Selling that stock on before it does make profit: pyramid scheme.

The fact you've overcome huge internal organisational hurdles to launch this product is irrelevant to the audience buying it, sorry.

Presume the opportunity needs to be MADE, not FOUND. It'll set you up better for the journey ahead.

Rising into the middle classes brings two emotional drivers into the mix: "I hope I don't fall back" and "I hope my kids do even better".

Remember that growth requires non-linear resources. 10% extra revenue might well eat up 80% more of your energy.

"Consumers always say the same things!"
Marketer ignorant of his/her products always having the same problems.

If you're not sure if the trending behaviour will continue, then plan for the other two options as well: stalling or reversing.

The biggest obstacle to getting lucky is presuming everything happens for a reason.

Charting future states without charting their implications for your business is like, well... useless.

If you want to see a stale team be creative, ask them to come up with reasons not to change anything. They'll have 100's of ideas.

"There is no life jacket underneath your seat. Nor seatbelts for when we hit turbulence. Parachutes, maybe." = Innovation reality.

Being able to see the merit of someone else's work and use it to complement or even replace your own, is a brave creative leap, not theft.

Someone probably already had that great idea of yours before you. Probably someone sitting in the same canteen as you every day.

The best way forward from your current position is making yourself obsolete. Simply because it forces you to move on and reinvent yourself.

I have a hunch that prosperity is roughly Bell-curve shaped. Not for income, but for the amount of trash you permit yourself to generate.

Arrogance: "I am right".
Confidence: "I can make it right, whatever happens".
Indifference: "Right, whatever".

If you create a clear distinction in your organisation between customer acquisition and retention, you will have equally disparate results.

I thought you did your 3-year plan last year?

Rank your own job's redundancy score:

$$\frac{["\text{other functions would prefer to get stuff done without me}"]}{["\text{who'd notice if they do}"]}$$

"Pfff. We can put a man on the moon but we can't get a live web stream to work"
IT nag overlooking we can no longer put a man on the moon.

"Has the potential to revolutionise [X]" and "Is revolutionising [X]" are two very different things, but continuously confused.

Hey leadership team, are you reading performance or assessing potential? Not the same.

Nothing distorts your view on the future more than what you perceive as your investments in the past. Your past self might have been wrong.

"The Schmeeting Point" - the point when more time is spent in meetings discussing what to do, than the time spent doing what is discussed.

[**Is your Innovation time line expressed in man-years or dog-years?**]

If Serendipity and Luck got the credit they deserved in business, there would be way less business books.

Water is a subset of coffee.

Almost everyone operates with best intent. That includes those b**tards you consider as barriers to your project success.

That unsettling moment you realize you can whistle along with the teleconference holding music and the robotic announcer sounds like an old friend.

If you're not sure it's going to annoy the hell out of your competitors, is it really worth the hassle?

I just learned a new word which I must use more often: "bifurcation". Wow.

"Less Is More". Try saying that to your shareholders with the same enthusiasm you're trying to convince your customers and suppliers.

Scoping or just coping?

The fact you disagree doesn't mean you're right.

Hey futurologist, technically you're not looking into THE future but A future. Note the subtle but important nuance there.

"It was one value-engineered step too many for me"
If consumers had the vocabulary to express why they turned their back on you.

The market research paradox. The more research you do, the more likely you are to hear/see conflicting things. Do it iteratively.

Roughly right is better than precisely wrong.

"We want to be as innovative as Apple." – Then you should make a plan to launch iTunes 10 years ago.

Isn't it about time to update quant survey Lickert scores to "LOL - OMG - LIKE - MEH - FFS - FML"...?

Being informed and being opinionated are not the same thing, either can be true without the other.

PROTECT THE INTROVERT OPTIMIST
AND SHUN THE EXTROVERT PESSIMIST.

If you keep your headphones on while asking me for directions, I will send you the wrong way, OK?

"Make Or Buy?"
The C-suite paradigm for innovation which too often defaults to "Make" and then fails.

**Hey SVP, do your innovation teams
spend more time preparing for
meeting with you or with your consumers?**

Assumption is the mother of all disaster. But that's just an assumption, obviously.

"There's no downside to this opportunity, it's incredible!"
An opportunity with no up-side either.

**In a shrinking market, copying
your competition is probably
not a smart thing to do.**

If you gather enough data, causality and correlation lose meaning as you can prove anything you want.

"Robust forecasting procedures" is an oxymoron.
If your system requires a lot of forecasting to run smoothly, it is clearly very fragile.

A: "The shame & blame culture in this organisation
    is absolutely horrendous!"
B: "We need to find who's causing it and fire them!"

There's no dreaming during sleepless nights.

The goalposts aren't moving, the field is.

Saying innovation is only about finding the right idea, is like saying you can keep an alligator's mouth shut with one hand and not bother about the other 15ft.

Half my fellow grads from 20 years ago now work in industries that didn't exist when we graduated. Makes you wonder what universities are supposed to teach.

If you're using macro trends to inform your innovation strategy, you're probably forgetting how micro your share-of-wallet really is.

It seems a lot of lifestyle businesses fear missing out on the Fear Of Missing Out trend.

A: "Let's ask a couple of total strangers for sign-off on our strategy."
B: "No f-ing way."
A: "Let's do focus groups then."
B: "Yes!"

The buck usually stops over there.

Judging by this stack of MR reports I've just scanned, Women's Lib must have happened in a parallel reality. It's all "Clean-Feed-Care-Repeat"...?

Mental note for next year's planning cycle: 'Hope' is not a strategy.

Creating, developing and launching in 8 months is pointless if you start 5 years too late.

"Women and children first!"
Marketing

"Not Invented Here" is absolutely fine as long as it's not being "Invented Over There" either.

"Reframing" aka "Deja New"

"Hold that thought!"
A guarantee to forget that thought. WRITE IT DOWN.

If you are category leader, then you shouldn't be awaiting the future, but shaping it. Actually, you should do that whatever share you have.

"What's the benefit of doing this?" versus "What's the cost of doing nothing?"
Short term versus long term views.

Sorry for my ignorance, but which of your MBA courses taught you "coupons" as strategy device?
Or was it as an intrinsic value multiplier?

In debate with R&D team looking for tools to save money on prototypes and need your help: where can I order a ruler with a half measures scale?

Inertia is not an external factor stopping you. Neither is paralysis.

"My predecessor was excellent and I have no plans to change the strategy, at least not for a while"
No one in management, ever

Innovation road map: Ask directions (*without shame*) / Straight on (*probably not*) / Correct course (*all the time*) / U-turn (*last resort*).

When dealing with ambiguous alternatives to choose from, it's less about what you choose & more about how well you stick to what you chose.

If you have to resort to crowd sourcing to find your company's next big idea, then you're not really in control of its future are you?

"Fifty Shades Of Orange" – A saucy new bestseller on interpreting mixed results from quant research.

If you're wondering what the CEO of 2030 will be like, don't ask today's CEOs to predict. Talk to the stars in today's middle management.

If you want to get senior stakeholders on board, make it sound like you're letting them in on a secret. Being covert beats being loud.

If you need over a year to sign off a foresight project, it has become an insight project. Another year, and it's a post-mortem project....

"Stage gate process" anagrams to "Sage protects sage", which then anagrams to "Greets scapegoats". *Remember, you read it here first.*

"Hidden development projects are no longer possible in our business, we have full transparency"
Someone unaware why 'hidden' is called 'hidden'.

We (*I*) made a unanimous (*polarising*) decision (*compromise*) based on observations (*hearsay*), facts (*opinions*) and foresight (*hindsight*).

"Business Analyst" anagrams to "An Unstable Sissy".

To explain your junior team member what to listen out for in focus groups, just say "WhatsApp me all the WTFs & LOLs".

Just to check, when was the last time you used one of your own products?

Few things are black & white in innovation, except for this: you MUST be comfortable with ambiguity.

Don't be fooled by political barriers being introduced as technical barriers.

Solutionocracy: the deification of people good at suggesting solutions, even when there aren't any problems.

*** SPOILER ALERT ***
Consumers have no idea what 'category' means, nor which one your brand/product belongs to.

Sadly, many global businesses seem to think that Developing Markets can be satisfied with Under-Developed Products.

Do not complain about your boss' inability to think long term if you've covered yourself in tattoos.

"Level five corporate leadership" anagrams to "Verified poser, all over the place". Remember, you read it here first.

Your number of options seldom decrease over time. They just increase in cost the longer you wait.

AS THE GERMANS SAY, A "WURST KÄSE" SCENARIO

The real-old Polaroids of Me versus the fake-old Instagrams of Me ... the Polaroid-Me looks real-young and the Instagram-Me real-old.

Wisdom Of Crowds: "Faster Horses"
Wisdom Of Operations: "Cheaper Horses"
Wisdom Of R&D: "Smarter Horses"
Wisdom Of Marketers: "New Size! Ponies!"

Are things really getting better or have you merely revised your expectations?

Murky Mechanics Of Innovation

**WHAT DO YOU MEAN?
THIS *IS* THE WHOLE PORTFOLIO.**

Murky Mechanics Of Innovation

Paraphrasing Albert Einstein;

> "Only a moron will believe that going
> through the same process twice will
> deliver a different result."

That paradox sits at the core of creating processes for embedding an innovation culture and capability into any corporation. It's real friction;

- Businesses want predictable innovation processes that deliver on the clock, at budget.
- Innovation is meant to retain relevance and deliver to a mostly unpredictable outside world.

How to navigate that gap? How come some businesses out there manage to pump out new products successfully year-after-year with process excellence and others fail miserably?

This is about balancing the Sunny Smile and Murky Mechanics Of Innovation.

The answer lies in understanding the different degrees of innovation impact. Too often, innovation is regarded merely as making money from new things for customers and consumers. What is overlooked, is the impact those new things have on the business itself.

impact on market

Game Changing innovation, new [product] for new market. Sporadic.

Stretch innovation, new [product] that generates revenue on fringes of existing market against new set of competitors. Opportunity driven, selective battles.

Incremental innovation, strengthens existing [product] and steals share from competition in existing market. A calendar driven, continuous activity.

impact on organisation

Incremental, change settings in the factory & update sales team. **6-18 Months.**

Stretch, find gap with new target audience, get R&D to develop new [product], order new lines in factory, train sales team and build relationships with new buyers. **A year or two?**

Game Changing, as Stretch *plus* develop new technical capabilities & IP, create new business model, build new factory, find new suppliers, replace personnel by new team with right skill set, create new distribution, ditch existing portfolio & its revenue stream. **OMFG Kill Me.**

Let's Look at these in a little more detail ...

Sunny Smile Of <u>INCREMENTAL</u>

Innovation to strengthen your proposition and deliver 'new news' along only one dimension, e.g. product. Most, if not all other dimensions remain the same. So you know who you're selling to, through which channels, at what price. You're innovating to steal share in well-defined market. You are probably already well equipped to roll-out these new products.

Because this is all about evolving minor tweaks within well-defined parameters, this type of innovation can be honed to a calendar-driven process excellence, delivering new products to market like clockwork.

But most importantly, you are doing this *all the time*, to maintain relevance to your consumers and please your middle-man buyers. From the moment you launch your product, you start lining up regular (small) improvements to keep copycats and competitors behind you. Ending only when the category goes extinct.

Another benefit of installing a good system for incremental innovation is that it's a great training ground for young innovators of all functions to cut their teeth, one dimension at a time.

Murky Mechanics Of <u>INCREMENTAL</u>

At first glance, you wouldn't expect too many issues here. It's controllable, relatively quick and low risk.

Yet herein lies the danger – because this is in effect 'innovation for innovation's sake', one can be tricked into thinking it's enough just to be *different*. It isn't, you still need to find improvements that are relevant to your audience.

Even trickier is when the process excellence team comes in, because they'll have a cost optimisation agenda to push. Not that there's anything wrong with trying to improve margin, but there will be when the benchmark is always last year's product instead of the original launch item. Countless premium brand products slowly deteriorate beyond recognition because their quality is being reduced via tiny 'barely noticeable differences' which stack up to 'dramatic drop' over a longer period of time. And then it's too late to turn back. A better way to deal with sweating assets is revealed on page 209.

Last but not least, because this type of work is left to the juniors in the business who are still pretty clueless of the product, the category and the history, they will rely heavily on models (e.g. research) to make even the simplest decisions, rather than good ol' judgement. No market research can ever beat experience and a night's sleep for good decisions.

Sunny Smile Of <u>STRETCHING</u>

Innovating to redefine multiple marketing mix elements you normally play with. This can be about approaching new consumer targets in new occasions, through new channels. You're innovating to grow the category beyond its current boundaries. You're probably doing this because the space you started in is getting cramped and you are starting to feel pressure on pricing, with private label products going head to head with you on quality. It is a sign the category is evolving into one where stealing share will soon be the only way to grow.

I dare say that the greatest innovators distinguish themselves by repeatedly succeeding at stretching existing brands and businesses into new spaces, just beyond where they played before. They take the time to find that new insight[6], source that barrier-busting technology and craft the perfect product-packaging combination. They care about exciting a new group of consumers they haven't seen before.

It's also a type of innovation that requires the most experienced team, combining creative & exploratory skills with commercial & operational savviness.

---

[6] *Not a fact, trend or snippet of data. Insight is uncovering a consumer motivation or frustration (why) with enough context (who/what/when/where) to generate new ideas. 'Nough said.*

Murky Mechanics Of <u>STRETCHING</u>

Pitfalls and bear clamps appear simply from human nature when you put different disciplines in the same room and ask them to cooperate. This is aggravated in Stretch for a number of reasons:

- Stretch is Opportunity-led rather than Calendar-led. The upside is that the opportunity is likely to be in an established market, which means it can be quantified. The downside is that you don't know up front what form it will have, so the importance & roles of internal functions won't crystallize for some time into the investigation.
- Functions need to work largely in parallel in the early stages, rather than the more sequential split of roles in incremental innovation.
- The leadership must be function-agnostic and empathetic to grasp the very different personality types and KPI's that drive decision making across the disciplines involved.
- The monetary risk that comes with the opportunity is often huge. More work needs to be done and big investments are likely for new manufacturing equipment. Leadership gets nervous and demands silly levels of detail for the value of a still hypothetical opportunity.

Clearly, it's a people thing. Stretch works well when you can get a group of people who know what they're doing to use their expertise differently.

Sunny Smile Of <u>GAME CHANGERS</u>

Game-changing, aka Breakthrough, is what pops up in most people's minds when they think of innovation. It's the aspirational activity of laying trails instead of following them. Fame awaits.

I suspect that this type of clean-slate innovation isn't Opportunity-led but Personality-led. When you're part of such initiatives, it certainly feels more like a movement than a project, following someone's vision of the future. It's why such projects are better ignited by a manifesto than a spec sheet. Clarify *why* you're innovating, breaking barriers, instead of *what* you're trying to do. More in the last chapter (p.257).

Looking for easy ways to define what your category game changer would be like? Two tips:

- Try the four TRIZ dimensions on page 23.
- Ask yourself: "what competitor's launch would keep me awake at night?" Then go develop that.

The major difference with both previous types is that game changers often require a new business model.

The reason start-ups can take on existing businesses is they have a product, then look for niche models & channels to monetize it where the big guys aren't in yet. Corporate entities work the other way around: they have established operations and look for ideas they can monetize through it efficiently.

Murky Mechanics Of <u>GAME CHANGERS</u>

Breakthrough is about re-writing the rules and creating a new market. As a consequence, any assumption on feasibility, value or risk will be largely guesswork and based on gut feel of a very small group of people. They believe in it. Great. The problem is there's no real way of knowing if they're right or wrong. History is littered with failures by people with *exactly* the same conviction and persistence as those who became success stories.

A cynical reality is that businesses that need game changers most, those who have Six-Sigma'ed their way to commoditization, will have no such visionary characters left in their ranks. You cannot process-optimize your route to breakthrough success.

But when eventually does all come together and you consider the game changer itself, *version 2* is the one that will work and make some money. Version 1, the launch product everyone is banking on, will turn out merely a proof of concept. This is always the case, check the history books. Why? Because the newness is so dramatic. You cannot create something completely new *and* make it operationally efficient or reliable at the same time. That's not a problem, as long as it's acknowledged up front and the resources are there to work on v2 the moment v1 hits the ground – probably by a different team.

! *Then you walk away from your ailing cash cows.* **!**

Pulling this all together

Great innovators understand the intricacies of these three impact levels and the difference in mandate and mind-set they require to complete successfully. They understand when to ignite each type, as well as to what degree you can process-optimise them.

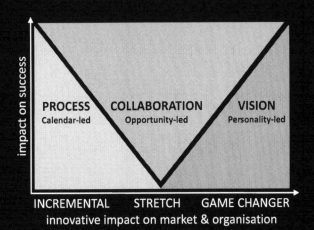

Looking at the impact levels above, one can see how 'Incremental' not only can, but *must* be caught in well-defined innovation processes as they guarantee long term ROI on innovation. But moving up to Stretching and Game Changing, the balance tilts to entrepreneurial. The processes that created the old markets have reached the end of their life-cycle and cannot deliver the breakthrough necessary to thrive in new markets of the future.

"Let's ask consumers what to choose!"
Someone who is...
A) A coward.
B) Ignorant to other success criteria.
C) Thinks consumers know how their business works.

Everything commodotizes, eventually. Everything.

There's a huge debate going on how to tune TV programming better to the interest of younger audiences. As if they still watch TV.

I suspect few people realise "wishful thinking" and "self-fulfilling prophecy" are inversely correlated, even mutually exclusive.

A change expert walks into bar
"This is all wrong"
"WTF?"
"You're analogue & you can't scale"
"FU & get out"
barman lives happily ever after

Be patient, time flies anyway.

Consumer research stating you lost on price
is likely to mean:
A) No real reason, you're just 'meh'.
B) They're fed up with the survey.

No matter how old & stale, some ideas remain new & fresh to people. Like the concept of remaining seated until the plane's reached the stand.

Wisdom of Crowds?
I'd say in the current state of affairs in the world, the crowds are the last ones I'd take advice from.

> **New movie pitch**
> **Evil super-villain invents unlimited eco-friendly energy source and then PATENTS it.**
> **"A license will be 100 $Bn, Mr Bond."**

A: "What did the moderator say to the plumber in the focus group?"
B: "You must be a lead user!"

Are you buying volume forecasting MR? SUCKER. Anyone who actually knows future revenue would be dealing on Wall St, not selling you MR.

Misunderstanding:
"Bankruptcy is OK as a start-up, investors value the experience". No, they prefer businesses run well over bankrupt ones."Oh you wanted a BIG idea?!"
Quickly hides pig under desk

Your strategy might be all about market penetration & building core, but don't forget at times your retail and distribution buyers just want something new.

The best moment to start working on that amazing innovation is about a year ago.
Same for writing that book.

Homeopathy was invented when an American coffee company accidentally made their brew too strong.

[1st Place Attitude] - [2nd Place Attitude] = [Ego]

If you've delegated direct client contact to a talking computer, you're showing your vision for innovation is efficiency, not service levels.

Hey SME leadership. When considering a country to expand to, ask yourself if you'd like to travel there every month before doing business cases.

Only people who regularly speak with their customers will be worried about losing them.
Come down from your tower.

When perfectionists consider their jobs done; in reality it's either too soon or too late.

(things that give me energy) / (things that drain my energy) = midlife crisis tipping point.

Hey marketer, follow the money. Parents with most cash to spend are those at the age their kids have left the house. Get with the times.

Is your breakthrough innovation really v2.0?
Or just v1.1? What barrier is it really breaking?

Anyone can plot implications. Only few oversee implications of implications and it's usually the team at the executional end of the strategy.

In hindsight, every innovation turns out to be just another halfway-point between what was before and what came after. Even game changers.

Hey Food & Beverage Innovators - the world has reached 'Peak Calorie'. Focus on getting people to eat and drink differently, not more.

In market dev context, many charlatans implies unevolved, infancy market. Maturing, commodotizing markets shake out the fraudsters.

At the table, or on the menu? Those are your options in a competitive market.

Perfectionism in implementing v1 works only if you've already started work on v2 in the background. No one-hit wonders.

The business equivalent of raising your chances of success is to flip a bigger coin.

I suspect Stevia was tested only as a written concept.

Entrepreneurial: accepts ambiguity in present, yearns solid future goal. Operational: yearns solidity in present, accepts future ambiguity.

RISK IS THE SCARY STUFF *OUTSIDE*
OF THE CONFIDENCE INTERVALS

Don't struggle downhill, that's just a silly waste of energy.

Hey Start-up, burning someone else's cash is not a business model. Sorry.

"Brave Visionary" and "Pig-headed Fool" are often only one feasibility proof-point apart.

"Dig a hole in the ground and run a train through? But the ground is for planting turnips"
Initial response to 1863 inventor of the metro.

Everyone, without exception, is risk averse. We just differ in the size of the risk we're averse to. Vive la difference.

The day you start believing your own spin, accidents will happen. Stay away from heavy machinery and don't drive a business until you sober up.

Have you noticed how founders of start-ups love calling themselves "CEO"? And never "Secretary General"? Except maybe in France.

Hey VC. If your model is hoping to sell hyped share to the next sucker, then you're building a Ponzi scheme, not a business model.

Here's a suggestion for a better quant validation score levels; "Failure" - "Risky" - "Ready" - "Outstanding" - "You Cheated The Model".

What doesn't kill you, probably almost kills you, therefore makes you weaker, more neurotic and paranoid for anything like it the future.

Note that when celebrating top-2 box scores, chest bumps are inappropriate. Save those for not being de-listed in year 2 after launch.

Fail Faster? Can we please agree Fail Less instead?

Launch in 9 months? Not if you can't register a new vendor in less than 3. Or send an email through your Citrix firewall in under 5 minutes.

**IF CAR DASHBOARDS WERE DESIGNED THE
SAME WAY AS CORPORATE DASHBOARDS.**

Hey Start-up, remember you're building a business, not a product. That nuance will largely determine your level of success.

[Even if you are not the category leader, there's no harm in acting like one.]

'Conclusions' are drawn from research, they live within its scope. 'Insights' are triggered by research, but are agnostic to its scope.

[Quant concept screening should include a 'pisses off competition' metric.]

Invisible & intangible system tech (internet) is more fertile BS ground for quacks than visible & tangible tech (engines, bridges).

Businesses innovate & grow their value themselves. Raw materials' value only fluctuates by scarcity & hype from others.

The only trend watchers you should trust are the self-made billionaire ones. And they probably won't tell you anything.

"Turn around, look back and see the best is behind you" < see what I did there?

$1Bn VC opportunity on offer: 3D printed drones that Snapchat pictures of taxis. You're welcome.

Categories where pricing's dependent on fads/whims will always be outrun by industrial productivity. You can't innovate gold.

With that big decision coming up, you'd probably do better with less data and more sleep.

Snorkels, gas masks, trumpets and referee whistles. Products that are all in dire need of real breaththrough innovation. That's a pun.

Ask not: "how much pain will it take before something changes?"
Ask: "how much good will create the momentum for change?"

$$\left[\begin{array}{l} \textbf{The scarcest resource in innovation} \\ \textbf{isn't Money, but Time.} \end{array} \right]$$

Hey VP R&D, Technical capability you want to excel at: develop and patent like there's no tomorrow. Because there is.

Riddle: **"Who pays for innovation?"**

ANSWER: Innovation pays for the innovation

If your category is segmented, consider UN-segmenting it for a change. You'll be surprised.

Coupons - vision, strategy or tactic? Discuss.

Intermezzo: Sh*t analogies in business.

Childish banter – yes, definitely. But in today's cross-cultural corporate teams, I've found fecal analogies* to be a great universal language for expressing and defusing Murky situations.

When seeing poor crisis management:
Don't deal with shit by stamping on it.

When you are dressing up a bad idea to nudge it past a critical decision maker:
You can't polish a turd. But you *can* roll it in glitter.

When you want to cut through group paralysis or blame storming over a failed process:
Passing this shit around just gets everyone's hands dirty. Deal with it now FFS.

When you feel someone is asking too many unhelpful questions about what is an acute problem:
If it's brown and sticky, it's probably not ice cream.

When you know you're about to be presented a dud: **I don't need to see shit in order to smell it coming.**

When someone is wasting time classifying a whole range of bad options, to find the least bad one:
Here's a funny thing about bird shit: you know what that shiny little black speck is, sitting in the middle of all that white shit? That speck is *also* shit.

* *Sources unknown, but brilliant minds no doubt.*

> **Breakthrough is about resolving category barriers, not your own manufacturing limitations.**

Big Data #1: "Measure to Control" - Yeah right. I've been measuring my penis for years and still can't control it.

Big Data #2: "You can't manage what you can't measure" - Which is misunderstood as that you should manage everything you can measure.

Big Data #3: "Live feed for decision making" - Your business will be in constant panic, unable to distinguish noise from signal.

Hotel Reception: where SUPPLY ("Let me express my amazing warm hospitality with a friendly chat") and DEMAND ("Just give me my room key now please") lie furthest apart.

Disruptive innovation pisses off the market leader. So if you're the market leader and you're asking for disruption, know what you ask for.

"New formula!" and "New recipe!"
The optimist's way of keeping a smile while value engineering.

Hey start-up, the VC is not gambling with his money, he's gambling with you. Just so you know.

"Now with extra [core benefit]"
The easiest and most overlooked way to create new propositions for your pipeline.

If you're innovating to grow revenue, don't forget improving distribution for some quick wins.

"MY EYES! THE PAIN! AAAARGH!"
First human pushing through category barriers to pursue the idea of chopping onions for dinner.

Wisdom of Crowds, or Wisdom of Bookmakers?
I know who I'd trust more with my money.

Did you know that hinged cell phones went extinct because of the discomfort for men with sideburns?

Yes, breakthrough innovation drives behaviour change. But if you're suggesting ADDING a step in the ritual, it ain't gonna happen.

Has crowd funding ever led to a sustainable new business? Or is it really just all one-off product launches? A bit like the movie industry I guess.

Figures should be taken figuratively. Not literally. Hence their name, 'figures'.

Cutting costs is not a strategy - it is a necessity after failed strategy.

WOULD YOU LIKE IT MORE
IF IT WERE 3D PRINTED?

PhD's that involve developing tools/products for fast moving consumer markets ... better speed up because 4 years lead time is too long.

Mass market essentials that have evolved to niche luxuries; vinyl, horses, fishing, V8 engines, C64 OS and pinball machines.

Hey, marketing manager. Had Twitter done what you have done in the past five years, these aphorisms would now be 350 characters, in colour.

To everyone stating that innovation is a linear & logical process - which ancient Olympic activity did Trampolining evolve from? See? See?

Hey start-up, it's not the quality of your idea that counts, but your ability to generate a cash flow.

Hey UX designer, consider your interface not an access, but a barrier between users and the product benefits. Your design will improve.

When your category/market is still immature, your innovation tactics should about differentiating from the quacks, clowns and frauds.

On transferring breakthrough innovation between categories; it's time that supermarket self-scanning migrates to airport security scanning.

A consumer panel recruiter walks into a bar. Everyone noticing the clipboard in time quickly leaves.

When you're clutching at straws at the fuzzy front end of innovation, it's better to clutch at fewer, stronger straws than more, weaker ones.

Reverse engineering stories around products that created a Paradigm Shift is also known as Marketing Bullshift.

If you don't grow the pond, you will deplete the pond, eventually.

Audits won't increase your innovation capability, but accelerate the opposite by chasing away innovative colleagues.

On innovation timelines
1 "Yonk" equals
5 "Dog years" equals time for
10 "Cows to come home"?

The fact not all shit-hot innovations from the US work in Europe or vice versa boils down to the Fahrenheit-Celsius conversion.

If you choose to create an innovation team merely to please the investors, be aware your successor may end up less pleased. So who cares?

"Oh no, you're doing it all wrong!" *All strategy experts, upon seeing their theories brought to practice.*

Whatever you think is 50-50 is probably 80-20. And your 80-20 is probably 99-1.

Break the category rules before they break you.

Type P-A-R-A-D-I-G-M then press SHIFT. Notice how nothing happens? I thought the same. Overrated.

When you set off to improve your consumer's shopping experience, don't forget to involve the retailer. What's in it for them?

A failed innovation isn't an innovation, just a failure. Which every innovation is, until it's succeeded.

Maybe letting go of your old cash cows is easier if you give them a full Viking funeral?

Stop whining about category intrinsic barriers. They're true for your competition as much as yourself. It's up to you to break them.

Category generic attributes are not a smart bet to build your proposition around. They're not ownable, that's why they're called generic.

Rather than ranking benefits, ask which benefits your target is willing to sacrifice for the one that really matters.

When marketers forget which part of their brand's heritage was true and which was spin, press 'record' and enjoy the show.

The more desperate you are for new ideas, the more likely you are to follow the wrong ones when they finally appear.

The difference between short term and long term innovation is improving a product versus improving a proposition. That's all.

"Wait, I really need to put more thought into this."
Engineer who really needs to make a prototype.

Build The Brand & Own The Copy

CAN'T WE JUST BUY THIS FROM THE SUPERMARKET ACROSS THE ROAD AND REPACKAGE IT AS OUR OWN?

Build The Brand & Own The Copy

Innovation in fast moving consumer goods & services – it's a tough world where the winners take all, right? Not necessarily.

Let's start by looking at the world of innovation through the eyes of branded goods companies. Looking inward, innovation is a difficult endeavour. It's all about juggling creative effort, consumer needs and technical capabilities; then convincing the channel owners you're the right partner to launch your grand ideas. You're on a knife's edge, finding the right balance between innovative leaps and operational reality, creating something new but not too new. Looking outward, it's a bloody war. Even if you successfully manage to outrun competition, your channel partners soon turn their back on you and start knocking off copies of the product you worked so hard to dream up and scrape a profit from.

Looking at the world of innovation through the eyes of a private label brand, life's not much easier. You manage a bazillion different categories under one and the same name, continuously looking for ways of improving quality and building the trustworthy reputation that will drive traffic through your stores' aisles. And just when you get that mix right, shoppers desert you for the discounters.

You might think: "It's all so unfair, with so many losers. And what a waste of energy."

Note that this is the space of Incremental and Stretch innovation, the supposedly 'easier' end of the spectrum.

An ugly truth driving both scenarios is that everything commoditizes. Nothing new remains new for very long and it proves that successful innovation is one that appears mundane in no-time, no matter how breakthrough it first seemed. Whether you like it or not, your unique advantage will be copied and move down the ranks of specialness – sooner rather than later.

Another ugly truth is that only innovation can pay for innovation. Whatever new thing you do, it'll need to pay for itself and earn back the CapEx you invested to get it made. You need to show an ROI quick or it'll simply not be worth the risk. You are always in a hurry. When the Branded and Private Label perspectives see each other as adversarial, that ROI timeline looks roughly as follows:

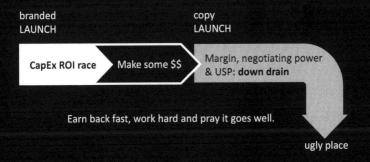

The Branded team launches a new product, then works like crazy to earn back the investment and hopefully has enough time left for making a bit of money before a Private Label copy is put on shelf right next to it. The only apparent solution is to run even harder on making that ROI happen faster.

Given it is virtually impossible to create products that cannot be copied, in particular in fast moving consumer goods & services, this scenario is painful. Not because of its unfairness but because of its short-sightedness. It's equal to ignoring, even running away from the inevitable.

What's more, the only possible next step for the branded team is to lower their price, which spirals into a fight that cannot be won. Red oceans are great for the underdog, not for the top predator.

The key to unlocking this conflict is understanding both parties' common ground: they both need assets to create their goods. The CapEx required to create truly innovative products is high, and in the scenario above is in fact spent twice; once for the original and then again for the copy. Not only are Branded and Private Label teams destroying each other's cash flow in price combat, they both start that war in debt. What a waste of resources, effectively shrinking the category value.

Dear Branded goods team: the answer is ever so simple. Own the copy. When you invest heavily in new assets to create new branded products, ensure you also own the capacity needed to create the copies that will eventually be made. Instead of hoping the PL knock-off will never come, agree with the retailers you'll create their copies after a grace period. It makes your future easier to plan and spreads your ROI over a much longer period. What's more, you can make agreements with multiple retailers and if there's one thing that drives down cost, it's *volume*.

Earn back at a normal pace, get the retailers on board for 2nd phase.

Dear Private Label team: accept that grace period and save yourself some money and arm twisting to get a high quality product on shelf.

What's the catch? There is none, other than that branded teams need to address their innovation cycles differently.

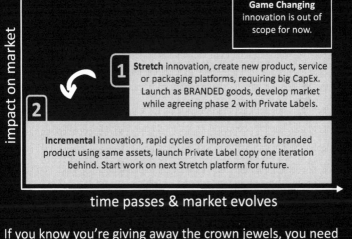

Game Changing innovation is out of scope for now.

1 Stretch innovation, create new product, service or packaging platforms, requiring big CapEx. Launch as BRANDED goods, develop market while agreeing phase 2 with Private Labels.

2 Incremental innovation, rapid cycles of improvement for branded product using same assets, launch Private Label copy one iteration behind. Start work on next Stretch platform for future.

impact on market

time passes & market evolves

If you know you're giving away the crown jewels, you need to have the next generation lined up and ready to go. In essence, you work on two innovation pipelines at the same time.

1. Long cycle Stretch innovation, creating the new standards for your branded product that require big CapEx investment. This is *literally* the next generation platform, the new manufacturing line that secures future relevance of your branded product.

2. Short cycle Incremental innovation, strengthening your branded product with small iterations. The moment the Private Label copy goes live, the branded product you're running on the same line should start receiving small value-adds. Sweat the asset so you're continuously

keeping your branded goods one step ahead and worth their premium pricing.

And then the story starts all over – but with more winners this time. You can even imagine a 3rd step, after a few years when the PL comes on board to the new platform, you milk the old assets for the new table guests: the Discounters.

>>> SIDE STEP ON SWEATING ASSETS

In the typical operational view on Sweating assets, the goal is to optimize production and cut cost out of the product without any (perceivable) change for the consumer. Which in practice *always* leads to iterative loss of product experience & quality.

A more productive and rewarding approach is to commission a manufacturing team to "show how this kit might create new features that add value for our customer without incremental cost". Or push it even further, "Where would you love to add 5% cost in this product?".
The response will initially shock and paralyze, as it'll never have been asked before. Followed by a suggestion to spend it on quality control, which isn't the point either. But eventually a creative engineering team will shift from a cost-saving attitude to the more rewarding value-adding mentality.

The culture you grow this way bridges a classic consumer-tech divide in many businesses, in two simple ways;

- Technical teams become skilled at translating features into benefits and vice versa, all the way through to manufacturing assets.

- There is less intention to commission assets that are 'singular' execution optimized, and instead choose for embedding flexibility for future product variations.

Sweating assets is often mistaken for a short term solution to resolve production cost issues.

WRONG: MOST EFFICIENCY GAINS LEAK AWAY AS ASSET UNDERUTILISATION, NOT MARGIN.

If you make products with 20% less asset use, but
have nothing to fill that spare capacity with,
you're not being very truthful to the goal, right?

On the other hand, a manufacturing team with a
value-add mindset can turn any production facility
into a sustainable, progressive, incremental
innovation power house, funding future success and
keeping the pressure on the business to move
forward.

<<< END OF SIDE STEP

A brave leadership eventually shifts incremental innovation responsibility entirely to operational teams, in particular circumstances where portfolio management is so heavily restricted by manufacturing guardrails, it is *asset* management that defines its success. Sales and Manufacturing are then in charge of the short term pipeline of products, connecting any shifting customer & consumer demands directly to manufacturing & delivery improvements[7]. Putting the short term responsibility for change amongst those who actually implement it also frees R&D and Marketing functions up to look at future opportunities that will drive the next platform-level technology. Win-Win.

That said, it is a brave stance in a mass market industry where MBA & Marketing skewed disciplines seem to pull most of the innovation strings. Plenty focus on strategy yet little interest in how their products are actually made. This needs to change[8].

[Insert Grumpy groan here, then have a coffee]

---

[7] *Ironically, this is how things are run in practice in many global companies already, especially those believing their global brand teams are in charge of innovation. They're not (our little secret).*

[8] *And it slowly is... SWEAT® & 'voice of technology' are playing an ever bigger part in the innovation projects we run with our clients.*

Maybe Homeopathic should rebrand itself as Nanoconcentrated or Hyperhydrated?

Then, just as you phase out production of the old stuff to launch your shiny new product, some client places a huge order for the old crap.

Hey Airline. When boarding a shuttle-bus to the plane, I'd rather forgo my frequent flyer rights and board LAST, thanks.

The first successful focus groups were run 2,000 years ago among 3x4 respondents (1 lapsed user) on a concept with 'faith' as only RTB.

"Looking for concepts with benefits"
Lonely marketer ad

The person who created your smartphone's autocorrect algorithm tested the concept in focus groups as "cellophane autocratic algae rhythm".

Think not: "How do I add a feature?"
Think instead: "How do I remove a step between consumer and end benefit?"

The "iconic" in "iconic packaging" is probably not what's stopping your consumers from abandoning you for better packaged competition.

Over 37%" or "Almost 40%" - framing.

Hey Recording Artist, if you want a truly global audience, get listed as teleconference holding music. Only problem is people will hate you.

Yo Momma's so fat she fills all quartiles.

Red oceans are full of opportunity (for the underdog, not for the top predator).

A Unique Selling Point for your product will be cancelled out by lots of Generic Disappointing Points.

It's easier to de-risk a risky opportunity than to de-bland a bland one.

Hey marketer, most female consumers are NOT moms. And if they are they have only 1.4 kids who bug dad too. Get with the times.

Don't walk into a meeting with your boss 15 minutes late while holding a Starbucks coffee.

My other $1Bn idea for cheap airline travel: charge $10 for a barf bag. Probably $20 would work too.

Note: 'hybrid' is usually the temporary compromise between the old and whatever little bit of new that will eventually be the new normal.

The fairy tale of service innovation always ends with them living happily ever after-sales.

The business growth analogy of building a car while you're driving it is incomplete. You're also doing it with a blinking fuel gauge light.

In the canteen of life, we all have a gravy recipe to cover up for bad cooking.

Are you moving your portfolio up into premium or democratising it downwards?

If you bring 'lean' and 'innovation' under responsibility of the same team/person, guess what topic they'll spend all their time on.

Americans are not worried about their privacy in social media. Just look at their public toilet stalls, they have no concept of privacy.

"OMG I AM GOING TO SLIP AND DIE, NAKED"
What everyone thinks, stepping out of a hotel bathtub shower.

If you have an international user survey to run, set up a kiosk at Dubai airport T3. Everyone's here.

"Buy one, get one free? How kind of this brand's sales & marketing team!"
No shopper, ever. The retailer gets all the credit.

If you consider your personal opinion as representative for your target audience, you're classifying your thoughts as perfectly average.

Warm-up and flex your mirror neurons before engaging in consumer research.

A super-power most marketers have is being able to jump to conclusions faster than a speeding bullet.

So you created a 3-year plan to move up from 5th place to 1st place? And what do you think number 4, 3 & 2 are doing in the meantime?

Somewhere, someone's making a living out of the exact opposite of what you do.

[Batman voice] The concept's benefit statement you wrote. It's not single minded.

I'm a bit disappointed to see this airport's six ePassport gates simply link through to a security dude with six screens.

Remember the Microsoft Office Assistant paper clip? I do. Regularly. Usually at night, chasing me in my dreams with unsolicited advice.

Cab drivers binary syntax for waiting times:
"10 minutes" < 30 minutes
"10-15 minutes" > 30 minutes

Descriptions you really don't want to hear/read about yourself: "Increasingly disturbing", "Harmless", "Pre-diabetic", "Loud" & "Too close".

Italic or Bold or Underline. OR please. Not AND.

LOW HANGING FRUIT IS PROBABLY STILL
HANGING THERE FOR A REASON.

Remember the days when you could boost sales with a "Free Toy Inside" without being told off for killing your margin?

Most products and services are a means to an end, not an end in itself. Which means people prefer less of it. Not more.

Don't worry about a decision tree for the people buying your product. Worry about one for people NOT buying your product.

"Designed in [country]" beats
"Made in [country]" beats
"Shipped by [country]" beats
"Mined in [country]"

Stevia is the universe's way of telling me I should cut down on sweeteners.

I think there's an opportunity for soft drink suppliers to absorb some of the world's excess carbon dioxide: "Now with 100% natural CO_2".

As kids grow up, emergencies shift from physical to social.

Screening out the bad ideas doesn't mean the ones you're left with are any good. Ideas must be developed, not screened.

Developers of wearable technology seem to overlook that the world is not 100% populated by hypochondriacs. Any non-health apps out yet?

Hey digital revolution, you cannot eat internet.

"TOO MUCH HAIR" & "TOO MUCH SKIN"
SOME LINKEDIN PROFILE PHOTOS

"Boolean Communication Gap"
When you say AND AND AND your audience hears OR OR OR. And vice versa.

An example of a message that packs both good and bad news into one: "Beards and tattoos are going out of fashion".

[great product] + [shit packaging]
= [untapped potential]
BUT
[shit product] + [great packaging]
= [pending trouble]

BoM rot. When value engineering transcends into removing value-add components.

NPD: "Now does [new thing]"
EPD: "Now does [old thing] better"

"Because it's [MyBrandName]" is a very poor RTB and an even worse benefit.

You can recognize anyone who grew up with MsDOS by their discomfort with spaces in file names. And they refer to directories, not folders.

Just paid $6.90 for a small Starbucks cappuccino at GVA airport and learned what price elasticity physically feels like.

"Operational innovation success" anagrams to "super-conventional association".
Remember, you read it here first.

Hey retailer, so your business model is to run at a loss all year through to November and then correct everything in December? Really?

"Stevia", not as sweet as it sounds.
"Steve" would be more appropriate.

Private Label teams talk about Discounters just like Brand teams talked about PL teams 10 years ago ("they're lower quality"). There's a storm coming.

Don't get angry with Operations when they scrap your idea being for 'too expensive' if you didn't check their capabilities before you started.

> **Don't take credit for a 1% upward movement of a quarterly sales figure unless you're OK taking blame for a 1% downward one.**

I suspect most people complaining about lack of good ideas simply don't know what a good idea looks like.

"NO I'm NOT too drunk to worrrk!" - the civil engineer who planned the roads to/from Leeds-Bradford Airport.

Probably the most anticipated automotive innovation for Mercedes owners is a feature that stops them being hailed as taxis.

Middle management is all about managing senior management.

Hey Market Researcher, how sure are you that your heavy users aren't just big boned?

Imagine your kitchen trash can asking "Are you sure you want to delete this?" every time you toss something in.

That colleague you think is a wonk thinks you are a fluff fairy.

"We need more chrome & wood!", said automotive marketing manager who needs a lot less plastic.

"Me too!!"
Most product launches

Viagra teams in Pfizer's corporate offices must have real issues getting their emails past spam filters.

World Procrastination Day, postponed again. :-(

Failure post-mortems: the vain assumption that although success factors eluded you, those for analysing failure are within your grasp.

The difference between a consumer 'need' and 'want' is expressed in the level of guilt felt in between consumptions.

1.4Bn cups of coffee are poured around the globe every day. That means there are at least 5.6Bn people with some explaining to do.

Ignorant Innovation Pundit Fallacy: mistaking 'Can Imagine' for 'Can Do'. Creating ideas is easy, creating business streams isn't.

**Inspiration didn't fail you.
You failed Inspiration.**

The middle word in "insight" is "sigh".

Your competition will thank you for promoting category benefits.

You say "neether", I say "naither".
You say "tomaato", I say "tomahto".
You say "top-2 box PI%", I say "small test market".

Ask any consumer for an opinion and they'll give you one. Not because they have one, but because you asked for one.

Youkea or Ikea?

"This product could do with a lot less salt", said the food brand manager tasting a prototype that could do with a lot more real ingredients.

The expression "back to the drawing board" only briefly evolved into "back to SolidWorks" and has now settled as "back to Outlook"?

> **Amazing how market researchers look for that one thing in humans that all humans dread being seen as: average.**

If packaging requires using your teeth to open, I think you can safely say it's a design failure. In particular for cleaning products.

The difference between "nosy" and "curious" is about 25 cm, or 30 seconds, or 10 dB or 1 question too many.

When space is tight, the sequence of your actions becomes important. Development budgets, car parks, political coalitions & holiday packing.

Engineering Algorithm:
LOOP(3;($PromisedDate+99);3DCAD($Ideas);BUILD($Prototype);BREAK($Prototype))+Flow($Tears)+FILE($Report)+HOME(5PM;END)

Lost in translation: "less trash" and "environmentally friendly" mean totally different things.

And then you realize you can blame EVERYTHING on the design team. Pfffew!

It's significantly more difficult to bullshit in Prototypes than it is in PowerPoints.

If you are hiring a lot of "Customer Retention Managers", then you are by definition hiring the wrong people, at the wrong end.

What is the complementary colour of brown?

"Yes this meeting room is hot. We're having a Bikram briefing session."

Hey global brand team, wondering how to make abstract strategy more tangible? Get someone with a local market P&L responsibility involved.

Great prank to mess up your Marketing colleague's concept scores: add "with free coupons" to the worst concept's benefit statement.

People dislike being average. They prefer being dynamic and exciting, aka a moving average.

"Whatever rattles is probably close to breaking." *Engineers talking about relationships.*

Tail Wag Dog

NO, IT'S ACTUALLY EVEN WORSE THAN LAST YEAR'S PRODUCT. BUT AT LEAST THIS ONE IS IN LINE WITH OUR STRATEGY.

Tail Wag Dog

This chapter is about methodology[9], what happens when processes & tools mix with human nature.

Let me get this out of way: *I'm not against process*. In fact, I absolutely *love* smart methodologies and I get physically aggressive when people deviate from paths I know will lead them to good solutions. I'm a sucker for frameworks, 2x2's and I spent half my career marvelling at near-magical manufacturing logistics that bring thousands of parts to the right place at the right time in the right sequence.
It freaks me out when creative gurus approach challenges without structure "and let it come".

The expression 'tail wag dog' refers to a small part controlling the whole, be it in size, importance, attention or action. Consider it through the lens of innovation, creating new things:

```
"The result will be remembered long after
    the process has been forgotten."
```

There's a clear hierarchy expressed up there. The process supports creating a result. A better result via simpler/less process is always preferable over the other way around. In that sense *any* process is a compromise, because plucking a good result instantly from thin air would be an ideal situation[10].

---

[9] *Syntax note: "Methodology" is the term I use to rake together all tools, processes, frameworks, etc that support delivering results.*

[10] *Many business functions are a compromise for direct access to whatever they deliver. Would you still use consumer panels as a compromise to research your market if you could also have direct access to all of them via the internet or so? What, you CAN?!?*

Process Excellence's main purpose ~~is~~ *should* be to maintain or improve the value-add & quality of an outcome, whilst making the process itself obsolete.

Yet in many organisations, functions, teams – even inside people's heads – "process" and "result" become mixed up and draw attention away from what matters. Fulfilling the process becomes a goal in itself, disconnected from the outcome it is designed to deliver.

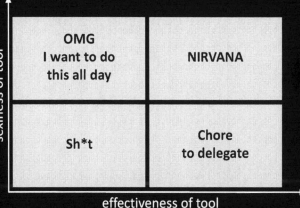

effectiveness of tool

If you're wondering if this is the case for you or your team, check your gut response to this 2x2 chart for Methodology Qualification[11]. If you are attracted mainly to the X-axis, you are a result-focused person and you are probably lying. You are much more likely to rank your tools & methodologies along the Y-axis, like the tool-focused person we all are.

Humans love tools. Even before we properly stood upright, we were banging rocks together to create utensils that eased our lives. Our resourcefulness is expressed by our tools. Today's (innovation) equivalents exist across

---

11 inspired by Darrell Mann's Steak-vs-Sizzle analysis

corporate functions and different abstraction levels. Tools, processes, hierarchies, stage gates, the ownership of which is often clustered in cost centres and staff functions.

So why are we such suckers for tools & process? Let's look at a couple of intriguing dimensions.

Personal Security

Tools & processes put a safe distance between yourself and the end result. More cynically: it puts distance between yourself and the consequences of your decisions. You can even say the process made the decision for you.

Also, you can blame a tool or process in infinitely more than you can blame an end result. Processes can be blamed for wasting your time, creating poor outputs, being imprecise, improperly validated, too wide or too narrow. But an end result can be connected directly to your decisions and actions.

Perception Of Control And Being In Charge

Our OCD tendency for control via tools is worsened further by technical advances enabling us to measure everything around us, right from our tablets. The fact you can measure it doesn't mean you can control it, nor that the information is supporting to better end result.

The perception of control is quite perverse; in particular in innovation where even at the most operational end of the spectrum (Incremental innovation) it is still a creative effort. One can for example be fooled that a validation framework to *judge* ideas is also suitable to *create* them. Creators use different thinking styles and frameworks from reviewers – and both are valid. The ugly part is that in Western corporate hierarchies, reviewers often sit higher up the food chain than the creators. It's led to the amazing reality that lower ranks are praised for creating ideas and the higher ranks for not stopping them. As if they're competing.

Perception Of Thoroughness

A process-heavy initiative will feel like a thorough one, with lower risk. Add in acronyms like PDCA, FMEA, RACI or DMAIC and we'll all expect things to be OK, in fact we'll even ignore things that are not presented to us through our processes and tools. Understandable for Incremental innovation when the calendar is on your heels. Yet quite counter-productive behaviour if you are engaging in Stretch or Game Changing innovation, where the opportunities must by definition come from places you haven't before looked, measured or analysed.

Collecting huge piles of data also raises the chances of finding large swathes of *conflicting* data, which confuses more than it enlightens. What were previously singular outliers which could inspire or be ignored, now become a statistical nuisance that need to be explained *within* the model.

Bad Before Good Feels Good

Humans are primarily fear driven creatures, as a creative consequence we're much better at finding problems than we are finding solutions. We enjoy it more too. When presented with a new idea, we revel in pinpointing all its flaws and then walk away into the sunset, feeling like we actually helped[12].

As a consequence, many processes and decision making structures are designed around evading wrong paths, rather than seeking the right ones.

Two examples to make that less abstract:

- Reviews after (innovation/launch) failure, aka post-mortems. It is quite amusing considering that teams who didn't grasp the requirements to succeed will confidently go about identifying why it all would have failed. But what makes the activity even more counter-productive is that it always ends with an *even stricter* set of criteria for launch, making success *ever more unlikely* to happen. Think about this one, it's a gem.

- Screening rather than developing ideas. Too many innovation funnels are purely selective, losing potential winners along the way because the whole package didn't meet expectations, rather than iteratively expanding the parts that do work over time. Where screening might work for Incremental, in Stretch and Game Changing you'll cull too soon and for the wrong reasons.

---

[12] *No, this isn't helpful at all.*

You Can Manipulate Methodology

Ending this journey downward at cynical depths before crawling back up; Humans simply love cheating the system. 'Beating it' as they will say themselves. Maybe not true for everyone, but definitely for the type of person working in a competitive marketing/R&D/operations leadership function in innovation. Processes are connected to KPI's and they are *so* much easier to manipulate than end results. The frightening thing is it happens with positive intent. All of the previous paragraphs show how hiding, hogging, hoarding, hitting and halting behaviours can be interpreted as being productive and serving the cause. Re-writing an identical concept 10x in order to get it past a hurdle defined by a quantitative test populated by a huge but non-representative sample of survey-loving people, ranking on measurable but irrelevant parameters? It happens all the time and with the best intent of following procedures.

GRUMPIEST POINT REACHED. FROM HERE ON WE GO UP.

Anyone with more than one product or service launch on their name will admit "Innovation Management' is a bit of an oxymoron. If anything, the innovation manages *you* and you just try to hang onto it and pass the finishing line in one piece and roughly in the form you had in mind at the beginning. It is a game of compromise, persuasion and most of all – the one thing that clogs all stage gates and processes – navigating **ambiguity**.

Over the years, I've found that the people most skilled at cheating systems put in place to manage innovation processes are *not* the evil ones driven by personal reward.

Instead, it is a special group that (at Happen Group) we refer to as **Innovation Rebels**.

For them, a Stage Gate is merely an obstacle course they know is part of the job.

The final chapter of this book is about them – hopefully you'll recognize a lot of yourself in it.

Free tips on next page!

Tail Wag Dog: Murky Process Focused

Looking across the spectrum of innovation, a few signs[13] of over-reliance on models and disconnection from the real world that drives successful outcomes.

	Incremental	Stretch	Game Changer
Voice of Mrkt Research	*Use 5yr old Segmentation*	*Single piece of research at start*	*Ask consumers what they want*
Voice of Technology	*Change product formats*	*Ignore off-the-shelf solutions*	*Test only internally*
Voice of Marketing	*Create new brand*	*Launch globally all at once*	*Rotate to new job <12 months*
Voice of Design	*Redesign pack AND product*	*Ignore category archetypes*	*Use old pack design*
Voice of Manufacturing	*Ignore Sales team requests*	*Go straight to hard tooling*	*Order high-volume kit*
Voice of Business	*Put accountant in charge*	*No market support*	*Drive for Margin Improvement*
Voice of Distribution	*Change outer dimensions*	*Launch in wrong aisle*	*Default to existing channel*
Voice of Supply Chain	*Remove value instead of cost*	*Exclude existing suppliers*	*Run a 6σ optimisation*
Voice of Boardroom	*Assume this grows market*	*Assume this comes cheap*	*Overpromise @ City / Wall St*

---

[13] *Disclaimer: this list is not complete, obviously.*

Dog Wag Tail: Sunny Result Focused

Attitudes and frameworks that drive successful outcomes in innovation, keeping a solid footing in the real world[14].

	Incremental	Stretch	Game Changer
Voice of Consumer	*Validation with Lead Users*	*Competing categories*	*Validate in real test market*
Voice of Technology	*Recipe changes with new claims*	*Trial prototypes with Lead Users*	*Be paranoid & patent*
Voice of Marketing	*Steal market share*	*Find benefits to tweak habits*	*New UX & habits*
Voice of Design	*No heroics on product or pack*	*Go for big shelf presence*	*Be a hero*
Voice of Manufacturing	*Sweat Assets*	*Co-supply new components*	*Run 1st year on pilot lines*
Voice of Business	*Clear KPI's*	*Involve lead customers*	*Consider Skunk works option*
Voice of Distribution	*Keep logistic parameters*	*Choose aisle with customers*	*Road test in new channels*
Voice of Supply Chain	*Co-develop with suppliers*	*Work directly with R&D*	*Up/Re-skill the team*
Voice of Boardroom	*Provide realistic resource*	*Don't get in the way*	*Have faith in Rebel team*

---

[14] Disclaimer: this list is not complete, obviously.

"Statistical confidence" anagrams to "facilitates disconnect". Remember, you read it here first.

> **Whatever the data says, it's still *your* decision.**

Dear inventors,
Big corporations are good at buying raw ingredients, people and other businesses. Not good at buying your ideas; they don't have a department for that.

So you had an amazing new product that consumers loved, but it failed and you say the market wasn't ready? Barriers are mostly INTERNAL.

'Consumer-centricity' methods are like harassing your friends for 'What do you want for your birthday?!?'. Don't ask, instead observe and surprise.

Knock knock!
"Who's there?"
"Would you like to fill in a survey?"
"Yes plz!"
Optimizes ideas for niche of nice people, who enjoy answering surveys

eCommerce suggestion engines don't offer you something new, but more of the same. You'll turn into a cliché of yourself.

Knock knock!
"Who's there?"
"Would you like to fill in a survey?"
"Hell no, go away."
Cleans data & corrects sample size to still appear relevant

Screw your 95% confidence. How about some "put your own money in this" confidence?

How long before a "temporary solution" no longer counts as such?

"Our insights are so good we call them WINsights. Get it?" - Market research salesperson about to be shown the door.

"That's not the kind of sample I had in mind"
Hands back cup to market researcher

"I. NEED. MOAR. DATAARGH"
Analyst drowning in data.

"Do as I see, not as I do."
Trend watcher raising children.

Really, are recorded customer service centre calls EVER used for training purposes? I'd prefer just training you directly.

I'M PRETTY SURE OUR PLANNING
IS NOW UP TO DATE WITH WHAT
REALLY HAPPENED

I'm not sure that 'ticking boxes' really counts as a result.

> **Processes are great places to hide in, even better than hierarchies.**

"Good insight, meagre benefit and rubbish RTB scores", said the market researcher reporting how global religions fare in a quant concept screener.

Captains of Industry have managed to create an Industry of Captains.

I think the world could do well with a "War On Error" right now. Too much stupidity around us, no?

"Hey, that's a perfect solution! And look here, another one! And another one!" - No perfectionist, ever.

"I probably already know the answer to this, right?" - What too few researchers ask themselves before doing more research.

*** BREAKING MARKET RESEARCH NEWS ***
Most consumers don't know their motivations either, so don't worry if you get it wrong too.

> **Shit forecasts can be recognized by the optimistic upswing being predicted as "just around the corner".**

Intelligence is less expressed through your amazing planning skills, and more by your actions when reality kicks your plan out the window.

In today's age project failure because of 'lack of communication' cannot be blamed on the tools. Not since the invention of the phone.

Data isn't analysed but interpreted. Especially when there's lots of it. It's OK, just be aware of the difference. There's a human involved.

Spot the Millennial by their utter disrespect of file sizes. Emailing 6Mb pics of cats and 97Mb ppts with only 8 slides.

Are our lives really more busy & complicated nowadays, or are research companies just adding that question to surveys more often?

Process Excellence projects should always have as ultimate objective: "Make Money With This Process While Staying In Bed Sleeping".

Tomorrow I must buy Uber stock with the earnings from my Groupon and Zynga stock. Oh shit.

Dear regulator, are you making it easier to hire or more difficult to fire? Not the same.

Whenever I walk in the street and see an electric scooter, it's after I turn my head and think "holy s**t that thing could have killed me".

I just scanned and shredded all my tax paperwork from 1996 to 2014. Does anyone need a big bag of ultimate piñata filling?

If you base your decisions on reports, be aware you're basing them on filtered, processed information. That's not bad, just be aware it is.

A 50% increase in innovation success rates doesn't mean much if it's reflecting a rise from 2% to 3% success.

If you work in innovation, stating you're a perfectionist is a bad thing. You need iterations. Roughly right beats precisely wrong, always.

Setting stricter KPI's after a failure will in fact *decrease* the chance of future success.

Has there ever in human history been an instance that someone actually managed to sleep better with a travel neck-pillows?

Process guardian:
"Secure, prescriptive & fool-proof".
The process executive:
"FFS find me a loophole thru this sh*t".

The fact you just received a 200-page market research report is not an excuse for switching off your brain/gut and believe every word in it.

$$\left[\begin{array}{l} \textbf{"My data is bigger than yours"} \\ \textit{Market researcher with small penis} \end{array} \right]$$

The simpler your solution is, the more difficult it is to convince others of its value.
Audiences confuse complexity with rigor.

I'm not sure all this fitness tracking wearable technology is making humanity any fitter.

I wonder how many market research agencies use their own qual & quant methodologies to develop new propositions for their clients.

"I will make big decisions on the likeliness that a paid respondent says they might promote our product to someone else, who then might follow that unsolicited advice and buy it, even though people can't even predict correctly what they will buy themselves when we ask them directly."
NPS in practice.

If you insist on doing innovation according to this long & tedious stage-gate process, plz show me the successes it brought you before.

Consumer segmentation. Or what the rest of us call Stereotyping.

The one thing I can guarantee Big Data will never predict, is the demise of Big Data.

Hey Product Designer, design is a means to an end, not an end in itself. If you believe otherwise, sign your work and sell it in a gallery.

I'm not staring at my phone, I'm checking the state of world affairs, OK?

Never forget that "market research" is a compromise for not being able to speak to all your consumers personally. A map, not reality.

Can someone explain me the logic behind Gatwick's Airport's Sky Bridge again? I forgot.

Complaining the taxi to the airport is more expensive than the flight itself? Take the bus to the airport next time.

In a 1,000 years BGY airport will be dug up by archaeologists and mistaken for a cologne factory.

BUT IF YOU *DID* GIVE A SHIT ABOUT THIS PRODUCT, WHAT WOULD YOU LIKE ABOUT IT?

However desirable it sounds, note that for whatever you track 'real time' it becomes VERY difficult to distinguish signal from noise.

Is there a process for being result-focused?

Put any quant market researcher in trouble by asking what type of people are willing to fill in 20 minute surveys. Not representative.

Quant agencies are insisting concepts are written ever shorter. Not for higher sales in market, but lower drop-out rates in surveys.

When you're lost, you prefer NO directions over knowingly WRONG directions. Yet in market research, the it seems absolutely fine.

"Who would like to join our committee to discuss ways of reducing non-value-add operational projects and processes?"

Has your Lean/6σ VP suggested ways to make his/her own team obsolete yet? I thought so.

That fact it appears disorganised doesn't automatically mean it is inefficient or unproductive.

Somewhere, some person is claiming that Big Data predicted all of this, in hindsight.

Hey Strategist, tell me about all the massive innovation successes you've ignited by stacking Excel sheet data. One example will do, thanks.

"Let's make this boarding procedure REALLY complicated and emotionally tiring"
Tourists on my flight to Spain.

"Yay! We're flying a 767!" - no passenger, ever.

By the time your operations make it to Six Sigma - don't be surprised if demand has shifted to an entirely different product.

"There are no bad ideas in a creative workshop!" - "Except for the idea there are no bad ideas!" - Two facilitators caught in logic loop.

Looking for some statistics, or market research on whether socks *size* correlates to how much *luck* they bring. Big Data, please help.

Paradox: one hides lack of results behind frantic activity, but one celebrates results that require only few actions.

Creating KPI's for a new product and creating the product itself are very different, yet often confused activities. #1 is talk, #2 is real.

If your job implies using a lot of statistical tools, raise your credibility by admitting being wrong regularly. It's statistics.

THE TWO JOBS *EVERY* CREATIVE ROLE HAS BEEN SPLIT INTO*

* *Inspired by Wulff & Morgenthaler*

The market research industry has a new way of mixing correlation and causation into happy BS aka "storytelling".

You will never have enough research for it to make the final decision for you. Ask yourself what the minimum is you need to keep moving.

"IF I CAN'T HAVE ANOTHER RUNWAY THEN I WANT MORE TERMINALS". Gatwick is what happens when you give in to airport planners' tantrums.

For market researchers, 95% confidence is good enough. Right up to the moment you ask them to invest their own cash in the project.

Something scary is happening in Operations teams everywhere, now that heuristics are being overruled by theory... Excellence Team, are you reciting business books or hands-on experience?

(Bureaucracy Impact) = (# Layers between you and any tangible effect of your decisions) / (# Decisions you make)

"Warp 10, captain? We'll have to wait for the FMEA team to report back first, sir."
Scotty, after TQM roll-out on Starship Enterprise.

"Captain, structural integrity is down to 18%"
Mr Spock halfway through Six-Sigma DMAIC and not liking where this is heading.

Hey UX people - well done on reframing User-Interface as User-Experience. But remember UX is still a means to an end, not an end in itself.

If decisions depend on nuances smaller than the measurements' margin of error, the decision making is the problem, not the measurements.

A Marketer walks into an on-premise, high-energy touch point, experiences a red/orange 2nd moment of truth and converts. <-- Jargon

When will architecture & civil engineering courses finally teach that white is not a filth & bird shit proof colour for buildings?

Calling it a 'reorganization' implies there was some level of organization to start with.

Market research credibility is defined by the n (sample) and money spent ($). Both must be high, the rest seems to be irrelevant.

Note that in every segmentation study, one of the personas is the SPSS waste bin, the statistical equivalent of Quasimodo.

"USE IN CASE OF EMERGENCY ONLY"
What the label on my hotel room coffee brewer should have said, to manage my expectations.

Cleaning the data? You mean change your perception of reality to fit your model.

The most amazing part of the news that the NSA has been eavesdropping French government data, is that they managed to decipher Minitel OS.

Clusters. They come in bombs, computers, SPSS analysis, headaches and f-ups.

Do you need lots of data or is one good date enough?

> **The fact someone wrote a blog post about it doesn't necessarily make it true, nor a valuable piece of information.**

"Find correlation, imply causality" - the cynical reality of most Market Research. In desperation to show value, the industry achieves the opposite.

Hey Six Sigma Black Belt, are you as comfortable working through 1, 2, 3, 4 and 5 Sigma using axle grease and a ruler rather than Excel?

The Trend Watcher Algorithm:
ECHO($OtherTrendWatcher);END

The Strategy Consultant Algorithm: IF($Reality)≠($Forecast);
CLAIM("Yes but"+RANDOM(NewsItem)
+"Not my fault);END.

High Purchase Intent scores? Be aware shoppers aren't even loyal to their own shopping list, before taking their answers too seriously.

The Data Paradox: the surge in volume of data generated globally is not from increased knowledge, but from being too lazy to be succinct.

Social media - where so many confuse being 'active' with 'productive'.

**I CAN SEE IT'S A LIFE BOAT.
BUT IS IT SAFE?**

"To slay a monster, we had to create a monster" *Movie pitch for the first action movie about ISO9001.*

The more complex the rules are, the simpler they are to bend. And vice versa. Stage gates, innovation protocols, regulation, corporate bonuses.

Data is NOT like oxygen. No one chokes on oxygen.

You can be 100% certain that none of the brands shown in your trend report used any of the trends identified to set the trends. None.

Market Research Movies

The Shawshank Regression	Bridge On The River Quantile	$\alpha > 0.05$ About Mary
The Good, The Bad & The Outlier	Variable Independence Day	Monsters User Community
A Sample Plan	The Binomial Man	Sophie's Multiple Choice
World War Z-Test	Django Uncorrelated	N=1 In The West
American Histogram X	A Christmas Correlation	The $\alpha < 0.05$ Suspects
Top-1 Box Blood	Graph Of Thrones	Mean Squared Streets
The Wizard Of Odds	Nemo's Key Findings	When The Bell Curves
Specific Rim	The Averagers	Rebel Without Causality

"Real-time Big Data Analytics" anagrams to "Amicably Agitated Latrines". Just so you know what to say when you meet a specialist.

A concept benefit that is so abstract that it is impossible to disagree with, will reap high test scores but has no value in market.

Luck, Patience & Being Right

I SAW IT IN A DREAM.

Luck, Patience & Being Right

Optimists and Pessimists will both refer to themselves as Realists, which neither are. When it comes to innovation, the Realists are characterised by their comfort with ambiguity. Where the Optimist presumes all will be Sunny and speedy, the Pessimist counts on a dark and Murky path ahead.

The Realists openly admit they're not 100% sure about what's ahead, but welcome the choices and compromises that land on their path – *while they walk it* – en route to a good outcome. They are confident to trust their own judgment and that of their travel companions.

This is the essential characteristic of a great innovator, crucial for achieving success in Stretch and Game Changing innovation. Being comfortable to make big decisions, or even change course, when you're already on the way because you know it's beneficial to the objective.

This is *fundamentally* different from what is expected of managers in large corporate organisations. In these operational environments the norm is to lock in all the 'evidence' at the start, chart a map of the whole journey up front and not move before a certain 'objective' parameter has been met. As soon as things then deviate from the map, which they *always* will, all energy is then focused on updating the map and keeping everyone who agreed to that map on board instead of dealing with the new reality itself and perhaps revising the destination.

When you're innovating to go into unknown territory, maps are always going to be incomplete[15]. Instead, bring a compass and course-correct when necessary.

Ambiguity seen through the lens of corporate management equals 'risk' and is inherently unwelcome. Which is why (at Happen) we call the people who can handle it well 'Rebels'. Their innate way of dealing with uncertainty goes against the grain of what the MBA-skewed norm requires, but it certainly raises the chances of success on the more radical end of the innovation spectrum.

Here's a nice visual from a Rebel friend on how the decision-making process differs. First the classic way of 'finding opportunity' in a business environment.

NO	NO	NO	NO	NO	NO	NO
NO	NO	NO	NO	YES!	NO	NO
NO	NO	NO	NO	NO	NO	NO
NO	NO	NO	NO	NO	NO	NO
NO	YES!	NO	NO	NO	NO	NO
NO	NO	NO	NO	NO	NO	NO

category parameter 1 (vertical axis)

category parameter 2 (horizontal axis)

- You chart the market along a number of parameters relevant to the category, ideally two so you can make nice graphs. In a food category, this could be as simple as 'time of day' and 'consumer demographic'.

---

[15] I have a hunch that more energy is spent on updating Gantt charts with hindsight than there is on scheduling up front.

- You spend time researching and validating each segment's business potential. This often involves quantitative research, asking consumers what they might need. The highest scoring segments pop out as what is worth pursuing with a Stretch or Game Changing innovation.

Now... This will all seem pretty solid at first glance and it certainly services the urge for rigour before diving in. But sadly, it's a false sense of security.

- The parameters by which you chart, are your own hypothetical ones and more likely to be business-led than by consumer need. It *appears* that you are charting a full map of the world. Even 'big data' doesn't provide patterns, only the confirmation of hypotheses you feed in.

- Any consumer research to further validate the chart is likely to be survey based and ask opinions on future, hypothetical situations. This means you're paying friendly people to answer surveys about situations they don't know yet.

Even more problematic: *it takes so much time*, which is the one scarce resource in mature competitive markets.

Then how do the Rebels do this? Well, I dare say *completely* differently. First of all, they start with a much less sharply scoped space to start from, at best an area of opportunity. In this fuzzy place, they start asking themselves (and their team) very simple questions (up/down, left/right, old/young, men/women, lunch/dinner) to *form an opinion* on what the opportunity really is.

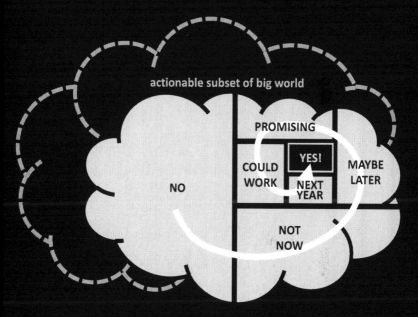

Rebels approach their innovation task much more iteratively, trusting their judgment on what will be the best next step. By this I do not mean they travel only on gut feel. By judgment I mean they are confident that when a fork in the road presents itself, they can decide then & there what information is required to make the right decision.

Why is the Rebellious, exploratory approach so powerful in Stretch and Game Changing innovation?

- Because you navigate iteratively towards a solution instead of parachuting down into one, you can always take a step back if your last decision turned out incorrect.

- You can start almost immmediately, you won't need to invest heavily up front in validation and – best of all – you need less steps in total.

- With less investment sunk in at the front end, you can walk away sooner and more easily if there turns out to be no business opportunity. Yes, *this* is what useful 'failing faster' looks like.

- No matter how virtually/realistically rigorous your upfront 'classic' investigation is... Because Stretch and Game Changing innovation imply moving away from your heartland: mistakes are made. The new territory is *never* like you imagined it and solutions will fail at first. Remember it's not just new for you, but for your consumer just as much.

Combine such an approach with a cross-functional, result oriented team from the previous chapters and you'll bring a bright future so much closer.

How to recognize the Rebels in your business?

You'll by now have made the link to the 'Personality-led' innovation I referred to in earlier chapters. Yes, these are the Rebels and you might now think this requires spotting the Bransons, Roddicks & Musks in your business at an early age.

Luckily it isn't.

As an agency working with the cream of innovators in mass consumer businesses, the past decade has given us insight and a surprising picture of what type of people consistently manage to define, develop and launch successful innovations. Winning streaks, not lucky strikes.

- **They know what luck looks like.** They are fully immersed in your business, have ears everywhere and are acutely aware when good vibes are in the air. Both in the market and inside the organisation.

- **They are patient.** It was a big surprise to us how so many of these Rebels are not at all the loud showmen & women we'd expected. Most are introverts. And because of their sharp sense of 'lucky' circumstances, they're fine to wait until market & organisational winds are favourable.

- **They know they're right.** They also know that when they are wrong, they'll *make* it right. That's different from pushing through an opion with a pig-headed mindset. It's *confidence*.

There you have it. Inside your business sit people who know where to look for the next promising innovation and they're patiently waiting for the right moment to act.

How to draw them out? The three characteristics on the previous page all come to the surface as *good judgment* of an opportunity.

When these people succeed once, they are likely to succeed again and again. *Acknowledge they were the success factor, not the system they operate in.*

They are attracted to the trickier ends of the innovation spectrum and the will find ways to cheat the system to make it work. In fact, they often *have to* cheat the system, which is designed for the operational end of the spectrum. *Allow them to.*

They are intrinsically motivated to innovate, which means they are more excited about results in market than being part of a particular group, brand or business. If their patience eventually runs out, they will go succeed elsewhere. *Give them space.*

The Rebels in your business are a prime case for successes in the past being your best guarantee for more success in the future. How to tap their value?

Simple: with **TRUST**.

But that's another book entirely.

To get stuff done, it's better to have a simple process and great people, than a great process and simple people.

[biz bureaucracy level] = 1/[biz trust level]

So George Orwell got the date wrong for 1984 by about 25 years. Now, does that make him an optimist or a pessimist?

"Google stops Glass development for looking too dorky". Bluetooth headset users disagree.

It's somewhat unnerving when politicians mix up the terms "consumer" and "citizen".

"You want a proven methodology, but in a form totally customised to your situation, of course."
The management consultant's daily dilemma.

"Our product is so new, we're inventing a new word to describe it!"
Innovation team getting ready to add "positioning problem" to their to-do list.

"My raw cookie dough concept is just way ahead of its time!" Indeed, you should have kept it in the oven for at least another 15 minutes.

"How do you measure a concept's potential to surprise consumers?"
Tiptoe-box Score

"Stand back, this is going to make some noise!"
Introduction to what can only be an AMAZING prototype test.

Anthropomorphism: Human capability that shows
A) our incredible brainpower
B) flaw that gets us eaten by animals with big eyes

Asking for 5 years' experience in social media marketing is the same as looking for one of Mark Zuckerberg's first five team members.

[
Are you spreading your focus or being selectively focused? Not the same.
]

That human tendency to translate "different" into either "better" or "worse", instead of just "different".

Great insight is less about looking for new things to see and more about new understanding of what you've been seeing all along.

Leadership vision can be myopic too.

[
Building relationships starts with giving, not taking. It's that simple.
]

"What?! This sausage is only 8% real meat!? A disgrace!" - Someone ignorant of their pension being only 4% real money.

Only in hindsight are there wrong or right decisions. In real life, there are only wrong and "seems promising" ones.

Putting a * in front of your LinkedIn profile name will indeed ensure you come up tops in my phone's contact list. But not for very long.

I sold my hammer and bought a clipper instead. But every problem still looks like a nail.

When Titans clash, fetch popcorn and wait until they're tired before stepping in.

The relevance of having 95% confidence in statistics-driven decisions depends entirely on the impact of the 5% chance of being wrong.

I suggest simplifying MBTI to two profiles when it comes to segmenting humans: Makers and Breakers.

Objective decision making? It's your neck on the line, not the data's. Use unbiased information for subjective decision making.

Don't go looking for 'objective' opinions. 'Unbiased' is a better angle.

Once your track record gives you confidence to explain things simply, you forget how much detail your audience needs to learn the hard way.

You ALWAYS have more than one option. The other option being 'doing nothing', which also has its benefits & costs.

"Opportunity" is an actionable subset of what's happening around you.

> **Anyone claiming a child-like mind-set is good for innovation clearly hasn't spent much time around children.**

100% Focus implies 0% attention to the areas where the unexpected events might help/hamper your initiative. Allow your mind to wander

The difference between an error and a crisis is the solution coming from reversing or forwarding the time line.

Coffee cup lids. Why do coffee shop baristas insist "because of safety", yet airline stewards not bother? I agree with the airlines btw.

> **If you've just suffered a marketing disaster, more marketing is probably not going to get you out of trouble.**

Hey CEO, the shelves your country MD is showing you on the shop tour look impeccable, that's because they cleaned them just before you came.

That trend report you're about to buy is probably more expensive than flying over and having a look for yourself.

Mountaineering: you want gear that is lightweight, unbreakable, waterproof and that you can sleep in. Like a simpler version of business travel gear.

It's the project post-mortem meeting that actually kills the idea beyond rescue, not the actions before. There is always a solution.

When your day's calendar looks like a Tetris screen, unleash the Space Invaders.

Maritime wisdom: you must step UP into a lifeboat. That's a metaphor for countless things in life.

You only live once - and so do the friends, family and partners who choose to spend their time with you. Don't waste their time, be nice.

At what age do you shift from trying to make your parents proud of you, to trying to make your kids proud of you?

For most brand gurus, everything tangible that doesn't comply top-down to their genius vision is a nuisance to step on.

I totally believe Google's self-driving car can handle Californian traffic. But I'm not convinced until I see it take on Naples.

HE GOT UP THERE WHILE WE WERE
STILL PLANNING.
LET'S REPORT BACK WE FOUND A SAFE ROUTE
GUARANTEEING AT LEAST SECOND PLACE.

Poolry ecuxeted idaes tedn to annyo poeple. No mratte how gdoo hte idae is.

The time of year that 95% of Americans forget that 95% of the Planet do not celebrate Thanksgiving.

Set ambitions, not as end goal but as reference framework to judge how well you're doing.

"I will also use this picture as my LinkedIn mugshot." *How many people brief their wedding photographer.*

**I AGREE OUR BUSINESS PLAN IS THIN.
BUT WE DO HAVE PING PONG *AND* AIR
HOCKEY TABLES CRAMMED INTO OUR OFFICE.**

I am a mixed-blood international entrepreneur.
Does that make me multicultural or border-agnostic?

Suddenly, I wonder why base jumpers even bother wearing a helmet.
Probably because their moms insist.

A 1-letter typo can make the difference between using and suing your regulatory audit team.

"Better to return halfway, than ending up lost completely" - Dutch proverb. Good stuff, those Dutch proverbs.

On a QWERTY keyboard, mis-aligning your right hand when starting an email with 'HI!' can lead to 'JO!' (good) or 'FU!' (not good).

True independence is not expressed in "money in bank" but "daytime naps per week".

To everyone who is about to turn 40. That's the age you can no longer be a 'high potential' and you have to start delivering the goods, FYI.

Step 1 in improving efficiency is building *trust*, not process control. Simply because it allows you to scrap meetings and reviews.

I can confirm that one downside of passing the age of 40 is that all your face's sweat glands migrate to your upper lip.

Contracts and signed agreements: if they are written properly, they can stay tucked away in the drawer forever.

If your first business value is "simplicity", I think having six more values on your list is pushing the definition a little.

I wonder how many EU politicians are truly aware that its economic, trade focused origins are what prevented wars, not its politics.

Hey Entrepreneur, ask not how to grow the business. Ask how to stop getting in the way of it growing itself.

Has anyone ever explored a correlation between Lego-or-Playmobil childhood, MSDos-or-MacOS teens and a Windows-or-iOS adulthood?

I have a hunch that successful artists are in fact successful businesspeople with an artsy hobby to fill the gaps between deals.

Youths' frontal lobes & planning ability don't mature until their 25th. Remember that when you ask them about their purchase intent in market research.

New metropolitan metric: UDOSOPK(x) aka Unsolicited-Drugs-Or-Sex-Offers-Per-Kilometer.
NYC: 0.2. Ams: 1. Paris: 0.5 Tokyo: 0.01. Shanghai: 5.

"I don't know" and "I don't care".
Correlation, causation, inverse-correlation, inverse-causality, or all of the previous? Discuss.

273

Hiring one CEO for $50m or two for $20m each. What's the better deal?

My shredder has just died halfway through processing my Xmas clean-up. I'm now wondering if the other half is really that confidential.

Frequent flyer dilemma. You're in biz class, your colleague in coach. Do you walk over and bring
A] Newspaper
B] Champagne
C] Smug looks

I can confirm eating sage is good for memory. I now remember I didn't like the taste of sage in my food.

I wonder if Amazon's suggestion engine eventually becomes so good, it suggests that one perfect book after which you're done reading.

[Pick my brain? What are you, a zombie?]

Planes, Trains & Automobiles.
BUT FOR GOD'S SAKE NO BUSSES PLEASE.

The only true entrepreneurial incentive for your employees isn't a big bonus upon success - it's taking away their house upon failure.

"Sophisticated" and "Complicated" are not synonyms. If anything, they're antonyms.

Serial Entrepreneur aka ADHD Entrepreneur.

I have a T-shaped consultant's shirt.

> **If you don't like the facts, then 'denial' is a great short term tactic.**

Hey creative guru, please plan your workshop out-of-the-box-thinking activities such that they only curl one toe at a time.

Successful entrepreneurship is less about delivering punches and much more about evading them with the occasional smack on the nose.

I prefer coffee froth over frothing coughs.

"YOU MEAN YOU LOST THE GOODS?!"
Fun thing to yell to your travel companion after you pass the airport sniffer dogs.

There are 2 types of developers. One believes anything outside their own expertise is simple.
The other empathises *all* development is complex.

Our new training program "Dealing with OCD" will start Monday or Tuesday, or maybe next week.
9am-ish, address TBC and no need to worry!

Product designers persistently present subjective opinions as objective facts.
At least fashion designers don't pretend.

Is Wednesday too early in the week to wish someone a nice weekend?

When "Genau!" just doesn't cut it, say "Wahnsinn!"
German lessons for beginners like me.

I knew London Luton Airport was nowhere near London. I found Luton Airport Station is nowhere near Luton Airport either. Luton, you liar :-(

Make sure you have its business card, before the opportunity walks off into the sunset.

When you agree something via video conference, aka "screen resolution".

You only live once. And so do the friends, family and partners who choose to spend their time with you. Don't waste their time, be nice.

"It wasn't me"
Opening line in all IT support calls and project review meetings.

Just had haircut, cut off enough hair to fill a pillow. But that's gross, so I'm selling it to a taxidermist.

Scientific approach to being an entrepreneur?
You mean you're setting up a separate 2nd business as double blind control group to disprove your hypothesis? Yeah right.

There's no such thing as "late". Only "too late", because everything else is clearly "on time enough".

If you observe poorly, you lose connection to the world around you. If you listen poorly, you lose connection to the people around you.

The Wise man knows when to shut up. The Leader knows when to shut someone else up.

You need a LOT of theory to dislodge heuristic behaviours. And that's for a good reason.

[**Do not mistake indifference for tolerance.**]

SU ~~MO~~NDAY

**YOU ARE NOW ALL INSTRUCTED TO
BE MORE ENTREPRENEURIAL!**

*** SPOILER ALERT ***
Experience *does* matter.
But you only learn that from experience.

My attempt to spice up my stroll to the gate with some Urban Parkour free-running is not being appreciated by airport security. :-(

Totally relaxed or total loss of decorum?

Cash flow is real, profit merely an opinion.

Using only one data source to claim you're right is only allowed if that source is your gut.

I'm in Dusseldorf. Which I had to explain to my kids is not from Harry Potter.

"Everyone always takes credit for my success."
Luck

Getting dirty is part of the game in any business; the question is if the dirt is gathering IN you or ON you.

If you insist on digging for a "reason why" for everything, then brace yourself for uncovering some incredibly banal ones.

[**Long term success is only granted to the few who manage to convert lucky strikes into winning streaks.**]

After
thoughts from a
GRUMPY
innovator

written & illustrated by costas papaikonomou

to Patricia, Spiro and Dimi
thank you for your patience with me in
the past looong twelve years

[**In the end, we're all just a persona
in someone's segmentation study.**]

After-Thoughts

In 2012, I published the first Grumpy Innovator book about the ugly reality of innovation in corporate environments. Then in 2015, I assembled a follow-up to outline why not all innovation is equal. In both cases, the responses have been heart-warming. Strangers invited me to present on stage. I found like-minded individuals operating in very different industries. It put me in touch with people navigating business risk in different ways.

Readers have been ever so nice.

- "When's the serious book coming where you share the exciting confidential stuff? I want to know how others mess up."

- "Please use more absorbent paper next time. I'm into cradle to cradle use of paper."

- "Did you draw these cartoons yourself? They're funny! But keep your day job."

- "Can you write something about small orgs too? Surely, they're struggling as much as us big businesses. It's unfair you pick on us."

Now in 2020, I thought it might be a good time to collate a third book and call it a trilogy. The first came out after we had gained traction with our innovation agency Happen Group. The second when we had become established player in the innovation world. Now we have sold the business and become part of a truly global organisation. A new stage, next life, new insights. A moment to take stock.

Also, the world has changed a little since 2015. Generation-Z is now well established, people bore us with memes and Fake News every day, and the next mega crisis has hit us in the form of a virus that is destructive biologically, financially and politically.

Regardless of all this (or because of) you'll be happy to know that I'm still quite grumpy. But less than previously, and perhaps because I'm older I feel an urge to reveal what actually works in this space. Imagine something between a TED talk, a coming out on Oprah, and outright lecturing.

I've compiled the following for you;

Premise: Why Innovation Isn't As Sexy As Business Books Promise

As a rule of thumb, there are only two routes in innovation. One is about sleepless nights, pain & hardship. The other is about sleepless nights, pain and hardship, plus divorce & financial ruin. This is not what the business books are promising.

Unfairly, the word 'innovation' is mostly used to describe with hindsight what someone has already done, and done successfully enough to get noticed. Winner's bias. Attention is skewed to the few entrepreneurs who hit the jackpot, not to the many thousands of people in regular businesses who create new products and services every day. Nor the countless failed entrepreneurs whose ideas brought them nothing but debt and ulcers.

The fancy chatter about disruption by start-ups with nothing to lose isn't much help either, when you're still at the front end of the journey wondering what to do next – with *everything* to lose. Besides, the chances of the world needing yet another digital platform Ponzi scheme that might succeed isn't very high. In all likelihood, you need to create something new *within* the tightly confined space of your employer's business model and market.

Should you then copy the habits of the successful businesspeople who smile at us from magazine covers and LinkedIn posts? Well, unsuccessful innovators show many of the same stubborn behaviours, so that probably won't work either.

Creativity gurus will claim you need to get out of your comfort zone in order to achieve new things successfully. The further the better – blatantly ignoring that most people tasked with creating the next big thing already are deeply uncomfortable with that assignment. If anything, *more* comfort is what you need for good ideas, not less. Long car rides and hot showers to let your mind wander, rather than your boss's ambitious KPI's to stress over.

A simple yet mostly overlooked first step up and out of that place of discomfort is to move attention away from what the idea will *be*, to what it needs to *deliver*. Almost all innovation initiatives are commercially driven by someone wanting to make money with their new idea. From start-ups to corporate giants, that new idea's sole purpose is to displace something else. Whether it's a small change to annoy a direct competitor, or a big one to overturn a whole industry, it starts with acknowledging what that new idea must *do* in order to be considered a success. Without that acknowledgement, it's simply impossible to adequately judge how radical an idea needs to be to make the impact you want.

Counter to typical business book arguments, you then want to find the *least* radical solution possible, because the less disruptive it is, the easier it will be to implement. A big reason so many innovations fail is not because the market won't accept them, but that they're too disruptive for the business itself to implement and sustain profitably. If the market wants a new flavour, don't bet the ranch by developing a whole new product with all the problems that come with it. And if you spot a very big unmet need that might overturn the whole industry, then you *still* need to find the simplest of solutions to answer it, ideally with a product or service very similar to what you're already making. The size of the unmet need being resolved is what counts. Not the disruptiveness of the solution.

If you're wondering what that means in practice, here's one example – and the only product example I will share – from our history at Happen Group. Working with a cough syrups manufacturer, their ambition was no less than completely revolutionizing that market. A very mature market, with established rules and dominant competitors. We knew we needed to find a *massive* unmet need in order to make such an impact, and the stakes were clearly against us. But we realized quickly a weak spot in most of the market research floating around for the 'cough & cold' category. It was all based on quant surveys and focus groups amongst people who were perfectly healthy and asked to *remember* what it was like to have a cough. No wonder no one ever spotted something new to do.

Instead, we quickly drummed up a few friends and family members who were *actually ill* and convinced them it would be a good idea for a few of our team members to come spend time with them. We tailed them for a couple of days and found heaps of unmet needs. Small ones, like the nuisance of knowing the sore throat is coming but not *when*. Or figuring out what kind of cough a sick child has. And we found the big one too. Or actually, a small one but true for nearly everyone: without exception, every sick individual struggled at the pharmacy or drugstore, when they needed to pick the right type of cough medicine. Was it a chesty cough, a tickly cough or a dry cough? We saw some cough in the face of the pharmacist, desperately asking "what kind of cough do you think it is?".

Bingo. Big need identified. Now all we had to do was *not* come up with a fancy solution. Not an app to cough in for medical advice, not a shelf navigation system. Our client made cough syrups for OTC retail, we needed a solution that would fit them and disrupt the market, not disrupt their own business model. A solution that would fully satisfy that unmet need of not knowing what kind of cough you have, easy to manufacture for our client and hard to follow for competition. So we created a cough syrup *for all coughs.* It went straight to #2 in the launch market in its first cough season.

Based on many years at Happen Group, helping teams innovate successfully in very mature and crowded markets, there seem to be four distinct areas that dramatically affect success rates along the innovation journey.

- **Clarity on the business objective**

- **Uncover insight you can act upon**

- **Create commercially viable ideas**

- **Energize the business into action**

Successful innovation in popular business media looks sexy and aspirational. You'll see in that list above that the ugly reality is that it isn't really that ugly, just a little less magical. More than anything, it's a skill you can learn and become good at, both on a personal and a business-level.

There's no magic ingredient here, just lots of good cooking. Let's dive in.

Costas Papaikonomou
August 2020

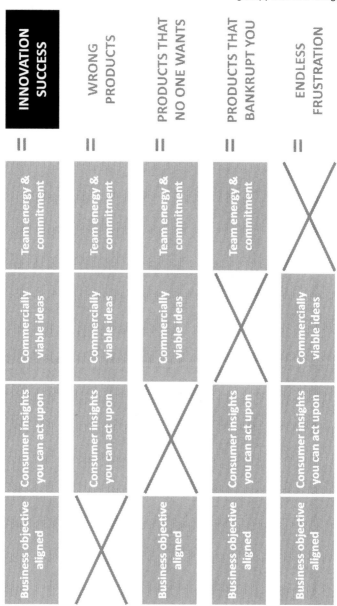

Never Change For Change's Sake

I KNOW OUR CONSUMERS LOVE THE OLD MODEL, BUT IF I DON'T CHANGE IT HOW WILL ANYONE KNOW I'M IN CHARGE?

Never Change For Change's Sake

Great innovation comes from clarity of what the business objective is, which the innovation is required to deliver in market. This is universally misunderstood. All too often an innovation project within large corporate entities start with defining the type of idea that is necessary, for example "We need the next [widget], with refills like Nespresso®".

Consider innovation a spectrum of activities, with a range of different outcomes: are you innovating to protect, grow or transform your business? By chunking it down to these three impact levels, each with its own definitions of success, restrictions and approaches to get there, clarity of thought comes much easier. For instance, one shouldn't try to create a revolutionary and expensive new product design if the business objective is merely to steal a little share. Equally, if the time has come to transform the business, one shouldn't be restricted by current technical (i.e. manufacturing) capabilities.

It might be that the over-emphasis of disruptive innovation in the past decade, combined with winner's bias, has made game changers all too much the benchmark for what good innovation looks like. The reality is different – managing innovation is less about spawning radical ideas and more about rigorous portfolio management. Businesses who maintain their portfolio durably over decades all judge well when it's time to create a new platform and when milking the old one will do.

The overarching principle that has garnered some consensus with is that ~70% of resources should be targeted on 'core renovation', ~20% in 'innovation for growth' and the remaining ~10% on transformational innovation.

So, how to set that balance? It's a fairly top-down conversation that needs to happen, tightly connected to the overall business/growth strategy. I'll skip going into the weeds of how this can play out across different brands, and call out the types of questions on should answer and agree upon;

- Clarify the business challenge to address for the brand in question. This is about being specific about what the portfolio needs to achieve in market, with your customers and consumers. This is externally focused. Not some hair-splitting debate on brand purpose.

- Agree the type of innovation required for which parts of your brand's portfolio; protect, grow or transform? Or NO innovation, which is an overlooked, very legitimate choice if things are in good shape and growing already.

- Be crystal clear about the target consumer and changing relationship with them that you're after.

- Review emerging signals of change that can be leveraged too drive your brand's agenda more easily. There's no harm in piggybacking on a theme that's front-of-mind for the people you are trying to please.

- Recognize the obstacles to success; R&D, people, channel, factory, politics, budget, culture. Call them out and adapt either the resource, or your plans accordingly.

"Yes mr Bond, this nuclear fusion technology could power the world 100% green, and before your eyes I will now PATENT it." – Blofeld's corporate brother

If you run a 1-person operation and insist on labeling yourself 'President and CEO' on LinkedIn, please also add accountant, typist, mail room manager and cleaner.

You lost me at 'EPIC'.

'Follow your Dreams!' – *winner's bias.*

"It's easier to commoditize something premium, than to premiumize a commodity"
* Contemplates brilliance of that aphorism while sipping a $6 cappuccino *

REAL INNOVATION HEROES
First person to dice onions for the second time
First person to wonder what aspartame tastes like
First person to consider an indoor toilet
First person to assume that wolf could be tamed

Do whatever you fear competition would do.

If you were looking to start a business in the transport sector, for about 8000 years your best bet would have been something with horses.

Just like the Hydra kept growing new heads, is there an analogy for something that keeps growing new feet to shoot?

In a shrinking market, the last thing you want to do is copy your competition. Instead: look for the gaps, the other categories your business has leaked away to, the unmet needs you've been missing all along.

Truly disruptive innovation looks like magic, at first.

Gentle reminder that at the time of writing of this book, the oldest Millennials are pushing 40 and have in fact become quite square - and fat.

Gandhi: "It is the quality of our work which will please God and not the quantity."
Data Aggregator: "Uhm yes, Mahatma can we talk for a sec please thanks.""

For a computer aimed at 'Creatives', why do most MacBook users keep the standard snow-capped mountain as desktop? Meh.

Every time you say Millennial, a Baby Boomer dies.

HEART (insight, why)
GUT (intuition, what)
BRAIN (technology, how)
Progress drivers are old as human nature.
Older than TED talks even.

Where GenX spends their lives looking for cheap versions of luxury shit, Millennials spend their time looking for luxury versions of cheap shit. Meanwhile Boomers had the luxury shit, and GenZ can't be bothered.

Paradoxically, it seems quite disruptive nowadays not to have a disruptive innovation strategy.

The real leader eats last.
The real frequent flyer boards last too.

Thought from a friend on how to act in life:
"Behave like you are an ancestor. Because you are one, of many generations to come."
Puts things like binge-watching Netflix as a hobby into an interesting perspective.

Recycling wasn't "invented" at some point. It was the normal way of life since the dawn of humankind, and still is, for everyone except for city dwellers in the past ~100 years. Who promptly elevated it to a virtue signal.

You can recognize the hardcore Zoom/Teams user by their casual muting/unmuting to insert a nonchalant 'hmmm'.

Niche, Nitch or Neesh? Asking for a friend.

Organisational change MUST involve product innovation. Why else modernize organisations around the crappy products that got them in trouble?

A tell-tale sign of a category still in its embryonic stage is the number of quacks and frauds still operating at a profit.

Forget about creating disruptive product formats if your procurement team needs 12 months to register and approve new suppliers.

Commodities don't go extinct but evolve into posh virtue signallers. Horse-riding, gasoline old-timers, scratch cooking, vinyl audio, meat-free diets, paper books and now even vaccines.

Whenever I hear a 20-something start-up CEO talk about 'fulfilling a life-long dream' I'm reminded I have socks older than that dream.

Places NOT to be rushed & hurried:
Operating theatre; Cactus farm; Domino toppling competition; Paris CDG

For anti-fragile innovation, ask yourself:
- Am I placing multiple small, low risk bets?
- Would a perfect outcome on one of my little bets reap something huge, or merely something small?

'Instead of WHAT will people use this?'
#ForgottenInnovationQuestions

If you always expect to fail, then you'll certainly celebrate being right a lot of the time.

'Age of Disruption' anagrams 'Aspired Goof Unit'

Divorce lawyers applaud countries that legalize same-sex marriage. Just imagine: 10% market growth overnight!

Wow. In a little chat with my local bakery owner, we realised he made $2.8 Bn more profit than Uber last year. He must be a good baker.

If words are not enough to convey the depth of your message, use Kung Fu.

Winner's bias. It's only human. Literally, down to every single one of (y)our genes.

IT Security Paradox: The more often I am asked to update my password, the simpler the password I create.

Given that eventually someone will disrupt your business anyway, you might as well disrupt it yourself, no?

** Innovation Conundrum **
Increased focus on breakthrough: good.
Neglect your core: not good.

Are ya'all still 3D printing?

'Turn lucky strikes into winning streaks' – the essence of good business.

Kickstarter idea: a Kickstarter function that checks if the applicant's idea already exists in better form elsewhere, and then orders it straight from Alibaba.

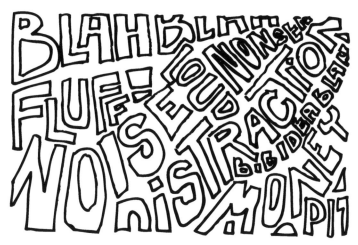

WHY IT TAKES FOREVER
TO FIND THE BIG IDEA

If you could go back to 2005, what would you invest in?
Tattoo ink; Gorilla glass; Marvel comics; Kale.

From a risk management pov, there's no difference
between carrying all your eggs in one basket or hauling one
massive ostrich egg.

Fanatics adapt their behaviour to achieve a goal. The
mainstream doesn't. Now think again about what your
sustainability initiatives are asking of your audience.

Accidentally typed 'Wealth & Hellbeing' and now I think I'm
on to something.

Beware of the competitor with
1) Deep pockets
2) Long term agenda
Because
1) = You haemorrhage fast
2) = You die slowly
1)+2) = Better quit and join them

When putting hypotheses out to field, please take care these are statements you could agree or disagree with. "I care about the environment" or "recycling is important" are not going to evoke a lot of debate. Include the trade-off in your statement.

'Fail Fast' isn't an excuse to 'Fail Often'

The innovation team's job is to make their business anti-fragile to the inevitable change in the market.

Most incubators are in fact outcubators.

Asking for a 2nd opinion because you don't like the 1st one doesn't mean you'll get a better one.

Don't talk about the strength of your brand if smaller start-ups are hammering you in the marketplace.

What doesn't help is that top-down intervention tends to be driven by belief that everything is top-down organised to start with.

The most realistic predictions on A.I. in the original Terminator® movie were:
- **Looking up a name in the phone book.**
- **Recognizing a face.**
- **Deepfaking voices.**
- **Driving a car, wildly.**
- **Shooting the wrong person.**

'Losing is the new Winning' – a dear (but anonymous) innovation friend of mine.

Moving confidently with little information: how experts and idiots operate in similar ways.

It strikes me how innovation teams everywhere seem to be looking for new ways of working. This is good. What is less good is the lack of interest in proven results of these new ways of working.

'Hominem unius libri timeo' 'I fear the man of a single book' – Saint Thomas Aquinas on fanatic readers of popular business books.

There are so many leaders courses on offer in my LinkedIn feed that I'm starting to wonder if there are any minions left to do the actual work.

Hey HR manager, before sending the team out on an Organic Mindfulness Rebirthing course, how about some basic PowerPoint training, hmm?

Sometimes it's good to pause to not think.

A brand innovation objective of creating "behaviour change" sounds to me more befitting a kindergarten or penitentiary, no?

**I SAID *BE CURIOUS* LIKE A CHILD.
NOT *ACT* LIKE A CHILD.**

What Facebook shows to business, is that the only way to win at the casino is to own the casino.

Hey Entrepreneur, *NEVER EVER* take advice on running your business from an academic. And that includes their books. Because: they're academics.

Want things to happen at the right moment? Initiate them yourself.

The difference between mere 'new' and actual 'progress' is that with the latter, you cannot go back.

Headaches are not caused by lack of Aspirin.

Hey Entrepreneur, remember: if you're burning someone else's cash instead of your own, you're technically not an entrepreneur.

Is it the start-up's idea that is disrupting the market, or the tsunami if capital behind it?

The difference between 'Game Changer' and 'core renovation' is 'Vision and Willpower' versus 'objectives and a budget'.

Opportunities & implications of platform design? Next time you see a Bentley, yell: "Hey, nice Volkswagen!" and you'll learn the difference.

I wonder if AirBnB®'s original startup VC pitch was: "We're like Tinder®, but family-friendly".

I suspect fancier tools lead to fancier dreams, not fancier outputs.

If you put your 3Y growth plans next to those of your competitors, the combined category would be 200% in that period. At least one of you is lying.

Heading home after a nice week in the US, a country where everything is doubled, tripled and quadrupled, except the layers of toilet paper.

Aha! We meet again, LHR-T4 G23... You devious little massive detour.

Game Changers destroy, before they create.

I've analysed this 2nd Tech Bubble and found the main difference with the 1st one is that back then, we all thought Hammer pants were cool.

Pray your competitors also have no time for vision or strategy.

Clichés. Annoying, but true.

A: "We should launch a game changer, now."
B: "Then build a time machine."
A: "Why, to steal an idea from the future?"
B: "No, to launch 30 years ago."

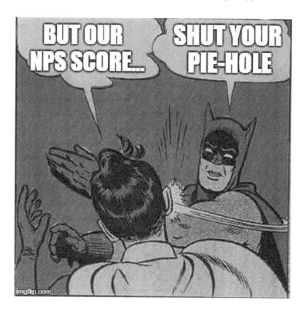

Nothing beats arguing with people who know what they're talking about. Because even if you lose, you win... new insight.

Is your 3Y strategy assuming a static competitive field, or a dynamic one full of people even more eager than you are?

"Build it and they will come" – what every innovator thinks deep down, even those with an acquisition & retention strategy.

Hey Manager, by far the easiest way to connect to the different pillars in the business is to rotate where in the canteen you sit for lunch.

Before taking any think-tank's New Year's predictions too seriously, read up on their previous New Year predictions.

The reason 95% of innovation fails might well be that in 95% of cases, a much smaller change would have been enough & far easier to achieve.

"What do you mean, there isn't a shortcut?!" – Generation Z growing up into adults.

Start-ups seem to be naming their businesses like IKEA names its furniture.

The only difference between "we want to be #1" and "WE WANT TO BE 3!" is pressing the shift key on a UK QWERTY keyboard.

Breaking news on "Well-being" need-state! It turns out to be "Vanity" in disguise.

Asking for disruptive innovation? Be aware you're asking to disrupt your business first.

Don't plan for change only. Plan for the new normal.

It takes a different kind of sales pitch to get people to spend their own money. Because spending someone else's money is _easy_.

It's quite depressing how "start-up" has become synonymous with "no viable business model" and that this isn't considered to be much of a problem.

Make the act of delivering game-changing innovation more palatable by first listing all the things you can keep the same. Quite a lot, usually.

It's national "Innovation Day" today. For statistical accuracy, every other day this year is "Failed Innovation Day".

Hey crisis manager: what have you undone for me lately?

"Welcome to the future! And again! I mean now, the future! Stay with me, future's here!" – Futurologist trying to get his timing just right.

Hey start-up, for the umpteenth time: the most important thing isn't cash, but cashFLOW. Make some money instead of just burning it.

Many innovations fail, not because the market won't accept them, but they're too disruptive for the business itself to sustain profitably.

Remember that your consumers' understanding of your category is about as precise as your own knowledge of say, the nuances of motor oil selection.

A mechanical design teacher once explained to me that 1 micron is what you smell on your finger after wiping with 1-ply. Wise man.

The only truly non-renewable resource is TIME.

"But we always do it this way!" – Organisational change team being asked to stop changing organisations for change's sake.

Hey Marketer, you cannot blame the audience for messing up your magic trick.

If you are the category leader, you should be the one setting the trends. Don't go searching through decks for trends to follow.

[
Bootstrapping.
The wantrepreneur's worst fear looking out. The entrepreneur's proudest achievement looking back.
]

For people using your services all the time, "Less User Experience" will be welcomed as "Better User Experience". Get out of their face.

Need an idiot-proof concept? Go talk to idiots for inspiration.

Don't bother revolutionising your own category. Too difficult and expensive. Revolutionise someone else's. Much easier and cheaper.

No matter what excuse you have, giving stuff away for free is not a business model. Because 'no business'.

Oil tanker metaphors often miss a part. Yes, they are slow to turn around. But once they move in the right direction, they're unstoppable.

Have you noticed how successful digital platforms are in fact examples of a back-office becoming the front-office?

If 'fighting boredom' is the angel investor's main driver, beware of excessive interference. All outside investors have an agenda.

"Ambition, Concept, Develop, Engineer, Hone, Implement, Launch, Nurture, Success, Win" – the sequence you'll only find in the dictionary.

Comfort yourself with the idea that competition is probably spending just as much time carefully planning.

Simplification is about letting go, not about summarising.

Turing redux: when your A.I. Device asks: "What do you mean I'm not human?"

Business models depending on suckers to fork out cash for products and services... Fashion, haute cuisine, insurance & most start-ups.

Hey CFO, if you'd reduce all your reporting to ONE metric for the whole business, what would it be?

Yes, it's π day today. Or if you're lazy like me, you prefer July 22nd aka 22/7.

Constraints, by timeline;
10 to 5 yrs: willpower/ideas
5 to 2 yrs: money/assets
2 to 1 yr: regulation/process
<1 yr: ethics/pain

"Research from your desk" – Probably not where the action will be.

Innovation Manifesto: brings ambition and strategy to life. Not to be mistaken for its middle-mgmt alter ego, the Innovation Moanifesto.

Adding home delivery service to your inferior product doesn't compensate for the inferiority of your product.

Please stop referring to app development techniques when innovating in FMCG/CPG. Different worlds with very different rules.

Consider every change a threat, you'll end up a paranoid wreck. See it all as opportunity and you'll still go nuts, but you'll be more fun.

And just when you're about to make it to the top, the top moves. Again. Bugger.

Things we falsely believe make anyone money: discounts, QR Codes, digital start-ups, web-banners, Michelin stars, Amazon, royal estates.

What makes decisions "big"
is not the size of the options, but when
"not deciding" is no longer an option.

Nespresso: a story of 30 years of perseverance with a game changer, or just no one brave enough to kill it after 20 years of struggle?

Redefine your target category such that it scares you again. Comfort kills innovation.

[At innovation project briefing]
Researcher: "It's important to keep all this in mind."
Practitioner: "No it isn't."

The fallacy of pursuing a bad idea because too much effort has been sunk into it to let go. If you'd walk into it now, would you stay?

In order to understand the thing you love, you need to take distance from it. Like a Greek tragedy.

Trade drives cultural exchange faster than marriages ever can.

Health: you don't miss it until you lose it.
Ambition: you didn't miss it until you found it.

"I will simplify this, just to show I was involved" – when most things start getting too complicated.

Game Changers. That doesn't mean you need a dramatic new format. It means you need to remove a dramatic problem.

Market leader, copying the challenger is an embarrassing sign you've given up & lost the game.

Evolve what keeps you awake at night – move on to bigger scary things.

"Quick, get me your cheapest heart surgeon, fast!" – Management Fallacy.

In a sharing economy, what acronym will replace FMCG?

Hey CEO, the reality is that merely protecting what you have will *also* require changing it.

Bulletproof or Teflon coated?

Struggling to define an innovation ambition? Here's one, free of charge: DO THINGS THAT PISS OFF COMPETITION. You're welcome.

Prosperity grows from embracing change, paradoxically the one thing prosperous entities slowly grow out of embracing.

Zoom in on any business success story and you'll see it's merely that their successes outnumber their failures by one – the most recent one.

Driving consumer behaviour change? Or merely keeping up with shifting expectations? Please be realistic about your remit.

I hope the next food revolution will involve un-revolutionizing the previous ones a little.

Disrupt someone else's category before setting fire to your own. How? Consider any of your business capabilities and see how they'd translate into an advantage by switching your business between these domains;
- Consumer
- Professional
- Medical
- Travel
- Education
- Military

Chicken and Egg
"I need to know the strategy to create future ideas"
"I need to know future ideas to create a strategy""

'Crisis? What crisis?' – opportunity focused person

Entrepreneurship – Now there's a thing society can never have enough of.

If you want to know how good/bad your competition is doing, place fake job vacancy ads in their name.

Quick, what's the latest on FOMO!?

That moment you realize how growing fatter doesn't create new empty space for tattoos is EXACTLY the micro metaphor for how the universe expands.

Circular Economy: ask the Inuit for guidance, not Harvard professors.

Paradox: If you pick a co-manufacturer over your own factory when you don't want to compromise, then you're setting yourself up for a long series of compromises.

When you introduce 'The Next Best Thing', don't assume 'The Previous Best Thing' is just going to sit back and let you roll over them.

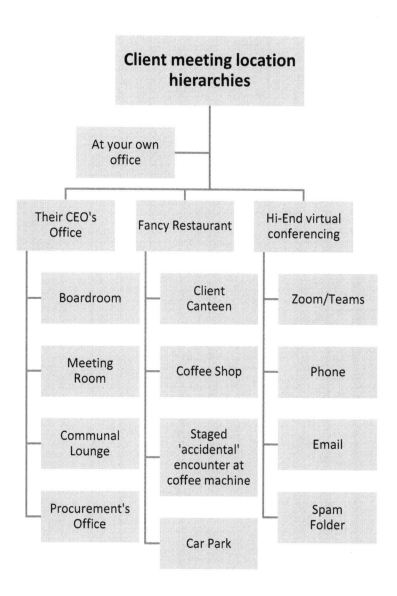

Follow the pain

WE INTRODUCED ANNOYING FLAWS IN THIS
VERSION TO GIVE US SOME IMPROVEMENTS
TO CELEBRATE IN NEXT YEAR'S NEW SERIES.

Follow the pain

Reveal real, unmet frustrations that will attract new customers to your innovative product or service. Too often innovation teams are distracted by industry truths and chasing generic trends or even common human needs. Whilst these are fun to investigate and keep everyone busy, their value for creating innovative and relevant new products and services is limited.

People will switch to your product only if it removes a functional or emotional frustration. C'est tout. In mature, saturated markets people will already be using a competitive product. Only their unhappiness there will drive a switch to your less frustrating alternative. Even in the dullest, most gridlocked markets there will be frustrations to resolve. The depth of the frustration you need to find is directly related to the business objective, in other words the innovation impact level you're looking to achieve. If it's merely snatching some customers away from your direct competition, resolving a small frustration will do. If you need to lure a whole new group of people away from another type of product and into your franchise, then you better find a big problem to solve for them or they'll just stay put where they are.

- Set the right scope and context to look for frustrations. This is basically a laddering exercise around the benefits that consumers enjoy from your product or portfolio. In case of a food product, is it taste, format, occasion, health, conviviality ... low down, you're comparing yourself with direct competition, splitting hairs over price, flavour and pack size. Consumers know how to judge your proposition, with a clear like-for-like assessment if you are truly resolving a frustration they are aware of. The higher up you go, the broader the competitive set of alternatives is, as well as the likelihood of having a strikingly different offer. But also equally less likely of being considered in the first place, nor it being clear why your offer would resolve a problem. Especially if your product is known for something completely differently. For example *"My yoghurt is the healthy indulgent outdoor snack!"* will need some explanation as there are plenty healthy OTG snacks already out there. The frustration might be a very nuanced version of health, while yoghurt isn't a product considered very portable in regular packaging. This is what *Blue Ocean Strategy*[16] boils down to, and worth the pain if the growth ambition is truthful.

Know where to look, how to look and go beyond the obvious. A default information source for planning where to play is via U&A studies (Usage & Attitude). Besides them being expensive to commission, they're so focused on the narrow category definition you already operate in that you're not likely to find much value beyond what you already knew. Besides that, your direct competitors are using very similar research. And don't get me started on the quality of consumer panels in FMCG for this kind of investigation.

PRODUCT PLACEMENT

Get the *first* Grumpy book for an overview of shitty research sources. Read the premise on page 176 now!

thoughts from a
GRUMPY
innovator

---

[16] Check out the handy Innovation Glossary at the end of this book.

Instead, consider using multiple sources, *especially* the newer ones like emotion analytics of consumer chatter online. Things people say when they're (un)happy enough to provide unprompted feedback. The gold dust of reviews.

- Whether informed qualitatively, quantitatively, once you made up your mind on the frustrations you will replace with excitement the trick is to progress to idea development asap. Don't waste time trying to prove the need is true. Proof comes from testing and trialing *ideas*, solutions.

All fashion trends rise and fall, except for tattoos which 'plateau'.

What is it with MacBook owners and that cloth they clamp inside? Neurotics.

Qual/quant consumer work – it's not meant to prove you're right. If you know you're right, skip all research and save money.

Are your products answering unmet needs or are you scaring your consumers into using them? Asking for a friend.

Understanding risk & path dependency: think of heavy drinking and using heavy machinery. In the right sequence, it's not a problem at all.

Set your research radars to 'super sensitive' if you want to chase noise all the time.

When you create a simplified model of a messy reality, the people using your model are unlikely to know what generalizations or simplifications you made. Your map will become their flawed cookie cutter reality.

I'm sorting & cleaning up my bookshelves and realize that I'd prefer to alphabetically sort my business books by title, and all the others by author.

All the coffees on my travel expense sheets are in fact cheap working space rentals. I tend to go for 1 coffee/hour/table.

IT'S ALL CHOCOLATE, EVEN THE WINE GLASS.
APPARENTLY, *THIS* IS WHAT WOMEN REALLY WANT.

I wonder if any of the world's millions of recorded helpdesk conversations actually ARE used for training purposes, or learning new things?

If you can move the masses, you only need to move them a little bit to create a proverbial tsunami. That's why most successful innovation and disruption is about resolving small frustrations for The Many, rather than big frustrations for The Few.

I don't think people change too much within their lifetime. But the societal norms around them of what's desirable or not shifts all the time.

Segmentation is in reality stereotyping, hard AF.

Market research and storytelling. Great, or awful things happen when combined. Handle with care, please.

Research Agencies spend fortune on shelf tracking & retail footfall analysis tools. Industry pundits cheer & applaud. Meanwhile, the audience shops online.

Of all the direct and indirect predictions that the Back To The Future series gave us, I'm still most puzzled by the manure dump truck.

Also, I'm now the same age as Christopher Lloyd was when he starred in the first Back to the Future movie: 47.

'I'm a celebrity get me outta here' – Millennials

> **Facts being counterintuitive > well, shit happens. Move on.**
>
> **Intuition being counterfactual > shit will happen. Stop now.**

I have a joke describing vegans, but really it's just facts and rather depressing.

On which page of your market research report should you reveal the outcomes?
A) 1
B) 10
C) 100
D) Suggest doing more research for proper answer.

Upgrade your segmentation research by calling it an Aristotlean investigation.

A map app for the moral high ground would automatically self-center.

To be brutally honest, I fear that for mainstream consumers Greta Thunberg is much less aspirational than Kim Kardashian.

Humans are LAZY. If you're looking to create behaviour change then remove a step from the process. Otherwise don't bother.

**WELCOME TO OUR FOCUS GROUP.
TODAY WE ARE GOING TO TASTE MOLECULES.**

I achieved peak-Taleb last week when I discovered my Kurdish barber also deadlifts.

Hey brand manager, don't go up into the stratosphere of emotional benefits and storytelling if your product/service isn't grounded by impeccable delivery.

'In my days [any activity] was so much more difficult' – older person talking, regardless of topic. And you know what kids? It's 100% true.

```
I wonder who Steve Jobs
quoted on his own slides,
when he was still alive?
```

A whole industry was built around the insight that HOUSE and HOME are not the same thing. A similar principle underpins most other consumer markets.

I'm boarding a plane that is three seats wide, yet numbers them A, D and F. I find that quite presumptuous.

Can someone remind me which Myers-Briggs profiles have no sense of humour?

I have a joke about statistics, but p<0.05 you won't like it.

Every successful product in market will do well in tests[17]. But not every product you test successfully will do well in market.

Hey Marketing Manager, remember you are not a representative yourself of 98% of your consumers. You're *way* more pampered.

Being 'consumer centric' doesn't mean every business decision should be delegated to a focus group. On the contrary.

I can do 95% statistically confident research on toilet paper using the readers of this sentence. But 100% useless, as you're not really caring.

To everyone ignoring 50+ year olds as potential consumers... they hold 2/3 of the wealth and they actually have the time to shop for your stuff.
Also, a 87 year-old looks at a 62 year-old thinking: *'What a baby, my kid's age FFS'*.

Big idea for qual research facilities: put some exercise equipment in the back room, so you can get some workout done while listening.

---

[17] *Because respondents recognize it.*

Innovation for Millennials. It's a bit like looking for presents to buy for nephews and nieces whom you think are too spoiled already.

Husband: "Her qual research job is outta control"
Therapist: "What makes you think that?"
Wife [through mic behind mirror]: "Speak louder please"

Crude math, but heck: with less than 5% of innovation succeeding, you can see why 95% confidence levels in market research is 100% useless.

Before submitting yet another explorative piece of market research, ask yourself how much you can answer just by reading the newspapers.

If the question "What am I going to wear?" is top on your daily list of problems, you don't *really* have any problems. Cherish that.

Cosmetics insight: once you pass 40, your face takes twice as long to unwrinkle in the morning. And when camping, twice as long again.

In market research, a high 'N' is in fact a token of low confidence, not high. To a confident innovator, n~5 is more than enough.

Of all the reasons why innovation fails, "too little data" is seldom one.

My sons have discovered their safest bet for pizza is ordering variants that I don't like... THEY WON THAT BATTLE BUT THE WAR AIN'T OVER.

"We're going to need Bigger Data" – if Jaws were set in a market research department.

As long as Market Research refuses to reinvent itself as 'spotter of opportunity' rather than 'manager of risk', extinction for the industry looms. Soon.

[**Remember your consumers would probably rather lose 10 pounds than gain 10 IQ points.**]

Market Research Prizes That Should Exist
- Best Enabled Business Decision
- Most Accurate Prediction Of Actual Market Results
- Frustration spotted that inspired invention
- Stereotype-free segmentation study

Guys, are we all looking at the same Big Data? How many Big Datas are there? Is it not big enough by now to be just one big blobthing?

You won't attract many new consumers to your product's benefits if you don't alert them of the frustrations with their current product.

Automatic paper towel dispensers. Is it me, or are they simply not generous enough?

YES IT'S EXPENSIVE FOR AN N=1 FOCUS GROUP,
BUT IS THIS QUALITY FEEDBACK OR WHAT?!

"The more data you collect, the more you can;
A) Identify conflicts
B) Cherry-pick
Research is intrinsically about building stories.

A: "... But is this where you lost your keys?"
B: "No, but at least here there's enough light to see"
Analogy for most market research

Insisting your volume of research makes your business on average smarter is like saying psychiatrists on average make smarter life choices.

If you think of your respondents like consultants... would you then still prefer to listen to n=200 average ones, instead of n=3 good ones?

It appears "you guys" is slowly creeping into the English language as replacement for "you" in 2nd person plural. And it sounds awful."

The significance of whatever makes you happy shouldn't correlate too much to the amount of happiness you already have, right?

Make any quant researcher nervous by insisting they divulge their source of data, ie the skewed, bribed panel they call 'respondents'.

The diet product sweet spot: are you more peckish than you are active.
The beauty product sweet spot: you are more vain than you are confident.
The convenience product sweet spot: you are lazier than you are stingy.

Interact with consumers to understand their frustrations and what's really going on.
Not to make decisions for you; that's *your* job.

Judging by the gargantuan size of most market research reports, I think "Big Data" refers to the output, not the size of input.

If your quant research supplier is explaining how you can achieve higher scores, he/she is only explaining how to beat their own algorithms.

A: "You know your BigGreenEgg® is just a snob's barbecue, right?"
B: "It's not snobbery, I just prefer the flavour of smoked over grilled."

High stress workforces in cramped, tiny spaces: Leopard tank unit, Apollo 13, Greek trireme slave galley and Caffé Nero at LCY Airport.

How far a walk is it?
Is it like only LHR5 A7>A21 far, LCY G22>G7 far, AMS H7>B28 far, or f-ng FRA Z11>A2 far?

"SIX guilders for a coffee you bought out of mere boredom while waiting for a train?!?!" – My 1992 self, disagreeing with my 2018 behaviour.

Hey futurologist, your sleeve tattoos kinda undermine your credibility for long term vision, no?

I spent all evening speaking with UK women about chocolate and now I'm wondering if I should feel surprised, enlightened or disturbed.

Processed Foods.
aka French cuisine.

My insight from all our work in 'home cooking' from this past year: the real threat isn't from new ways of cooking, but not cooking at all.

Once you have a hypothesis, data transforms into evidence. Otherwise it's just words & numbers.

A: "Plz recruit users of product X and Y"
B: "We can't, incidence is too low :-("
A: "OK, only X users then"
Hope flies out of window

The real reason many marketers prefer quant research over test launches, even at the lower cost and speed, is you can't cheat in test launches.

"Consumer Co-creation" – the methodology that created classics like The Edsel, New Coke, The Millennium Dome, BK Crispy Fries and Boaty McBoatface.

Show me a consumer who asks for 'disruption' and I'll show you an anarchist maniac. The word doesn't mean to them what it means to you.

There comes a point your research iterations are so close together you're just chasing noise, not a signal.

If you know the viewing facility's food menu by heart, it's time to move to another research methodology, not another venue.

Looking to commission an 'infographic' to sauce up your data? Make sure the designer actually understands the data or it'll just be a mess.

Decisions should eventually be based on n=1. The 1 being the person who deals with the consequences.

Rate how much you love your partner on a Lickert scale and you'll find that:
1) Lickert scales don't work
2) It's a little creepy too

Meta-question: will a survey among n=1,000 market researchers reveal the true state of the market research industry? I'm not so sure.

"Mirror Mirror on the wall, who's the prettiest of them all?" – Focus group viewing rooms, every day.

Focus group viewing facilities ... where people on both sides of the mirror pretend they care.

> **Twice the amount of data will also give you twice the amount of conflicting data.**

While your shopper- and consumer-insights-manager bicker over who owns that part of the journey, your real audience switches to competition.

I had a project conversation about Xylitol that was so passionate I think there's good material for a musical in there.

> **To the teams developing all these new market research tools: without improving the shoddy underlying respondent panels, it's like developing fancy apps for BlackBerry OS.**

Successful writers do not "co-create" books with their readers. So when co-creating with consumers, know your role & responsibility vs theirs.

"We can't possibly make our product premium :-(" – says Marketing Manager, then takes a sip from a $3/250ml bottle of water.

'Specialist' doesn't mean 'very good' or 'expert'. it means 'narrow focus'. Keep that in mind when picking your job title, or hiring specialists.

Wife: "His job in market research is taking over our marriage."
Therapist: "Sir, what do you have to say about that?"
Husband: "Typical over-indexing for her Extravert Controller persona."

Candy packaging paradox: fun size is the least fun.

Mansplaining sports injuries by 40+ year old males: "Clearly, my gear wasn't expensive enough. And I need more of it".

*** SPOILER ALERT ***
The moment Millennials have children, they become as square as every generation before them. Maybe even squarer."

"Total Addressable Market" – Interesting definition for postal logistics companies and internet dating.

Only market researchers can get away with outright discriminatory statements about segmentation, lead users & hi-relevance consumers.

Wife: "He's only interested in numbers, thinks in-the-box, always late and I can't rely on his advice" BFF: "Leave him. It's a Usage & Attitude problem"

Swiping an iPhone as wireless clicker for a PowerPoint presentation? About as pompous as saying 'next slide' to your Google Glasses.

On fancy food ingredients. Be aware that many people think a calorie is an ingredient, and full-fat milk is 100% fat. Etcetera ignorance.

Funny how young kids think milk is made in the supermarket, while we all know it's made by home delivery companies.

"Optimism Bias" – what gets difficult stuff done.

Qual vs Quant, aka Opinions vs Statistics.
Both are bendable, subjective & fallible.

The Bored act in mysterious ways.

Things with no value are seldom free.

Sadly, it's far more difficult to build a case on your deep understanding of consumers, than on a direct quote from some random person in the street.

"Let your gut guide you, not the guide gut you." – Mohammed Ali's focus group moderator friend.

"Island Time" – A mindset, independent of topography or time.

Science is about proving you're wrong, Market Research is about proving you're right. Not the same, sorry.

Hey Gen-X, wondering why Millennials are so odd? Then just imagine what you'd have done to fight the boredom taking 10 more years to grow up.

"Take me to your leader." – trend spotter

KnockKnock
Who's there?
Semi
Semi Who?
Semi Monadic
KnockKnock KnockKnock KnockKnock KnockKnock
KnockKnock KnockKnock KnockKnock

Logging on through Citrix ... you just know the software on the other side is not going to deliver an enjoyable user experience.

The fact you are a Regular/Heavy User of toilet paper doesn't mean you have interesting opinions about it. Lapsed Users on the other hand...

NPS survey reports sound like cheesy dating shows.

"Sharing Economy" ... is that Millennial-speak for being broke?

If you want to understand the different in digital privacy laws between the US, Europe and China, just visit a local public toilet.

Passing between me and my luggage is like walking between Mama Bear and her cubs.

Jackson Pollock was so ahead of his time: just look at his Big Data infographics as early as the 1940's.

How do you best treat an anomaly in your research?
A) Explain with fuzzy statistics
B) Kill with fire
C) Celebrate

> **Archive reports don't talk back, nor get angry when you disagree with them. That's why they're way too comfortable for using as sole base for your work.**

If you don't believe disgust and desire can go hand in hand... imagine the person next to you on the train eating a kebab.

As a rule of thumb, presume your consumers care about 95% less about your products than you do. Just to manage expectations.

The problem with having too much data is that you feel extra stupid not to be able to make sense of it.

Personality tests. Remind me again which Myers-Briggs type was the one that doesn't get sarcasm?

Last week's Fortnite championships show the coming of age of Generation Z, the watershed moment that Millennials realize they can join us Gen-X'ers in the league of irrelevant 'has beens'.

> **PPTs: Very Narrow textboxes are a nuisance to read Please choose smaller font size or widen box. Thank you.**

Lickert scales in market research can be simplified to a Y/N question: 'is this badass or not?' Seriously, excitement is all you need.

Isn't it incredible how Generation-Z is stealing Millennials' limelight with genuinely nicer interests? Sustainability and saving the planet, rather than gastro-burgers and selfies. There is hope for mankind.

Your response to fresh snow reveals your mental age.

Remember that only 3-4 years ago, our biggest concern was whether we were hydrated enough.

In business data analysis ... flashy analysis is used to mask poor quality data. Good data speaks for itself.

Heuristic: never take dietary advice from anyone under 40. Make that 50.

Trend agencies regurgitate selectively from the past. If they could predict the future, they'd be the richest businesses ever. They're not.

Eye Tracker MR: "I will allow researchers to post-rationalize design decisions ad infinitum"
Neuro MR: "Hold my beer"

People do not want to be 'educated' about the tech enabling your product. Just like you don't want to be educated about things like motor oil and pet insurance.

Sometimes a stock photo says more than a 1,000 words. But it usually just says "stock photo".

Dear FMCG innovation person, please don't forget to use your own products every now and then, even if you're not the target audience. Tool Wag Dog.
Aka Methodolorgy.

If you do Market Research only to convince internal stakeholders, you'd better just spend that money on wining, dining or bribing them.

Can someone remind me which Myers-Briggs profiles tend to blow the family fortune? Or was it a nurture/nature thing?

There is brooooaaad grey area between an attempt to make technology exciting for the masses and tapping a pool of gullible nerds who buy everything.

Logic and narrative form our stories of our Past, and musings about our Future. Yet in transit through the Now, they temporarily vanish.

Given the peculiar position in which many people hold their phones nowadays, I suggest phone designers look at pizza slices for inspiration.

The ancient Greeks identified 4 personality types, fully intertwined with environment. Farmers, City people, Warriors and Mountain people. Because they understood context and character are indivisible.

The Salmon. Aka the person disembarking from a plane who first needs to fetch hand luggage from bin at higher seat row.

I estimate that 87.3% of statistics present a false level of accuracy.

Sometimes the Bull's Eye Consumer is so specific they're even less likely to exist than the Perfectly Average Consumer.

My sons' maths and fractions skills improve dramatically when I apply it to how much of their pizza I want to claim.

IF THIS IS YOUR SHELF DISPLAY
YOU NEED CHOPPER INSIGHT

Maybe we need more Consumer Segment Personas?" – Such a typical Stressed Structure Seeker thing to say.

BAR MENU

== TODAY'S CHEESY SPECIALS ==

```
[A Procurement Manager walks into a bar]
"I want a discount on my beer!"
"No problem."
[Barman serves smaller beer]
```

```
[A man walks into a Bay Area Start-up Bar]
"I'd like 2,500 free craft beers please."
"Sure, if you Instagram them."
[Barman sells bar for $200m]
```

```
[Risk Analyst walks into a bar]
"You know you're risking your health here,
right?"
"You know you're risking yours saying that here,
right?"
[Business continues as normal]
```

```
[The Bar franchise CEO plans tour of the
premises]
[Barman tidies up bar, wipes tables & kicks out
drunk patrons]
CEO: "See? Our bars look nice."
```

Table 344

[An Operations analyst walks into a bar]
"If you pre-fill your beer glasses in the daytime lull, you'll achieve a 30% better tap utilization during evening rush hour"
[Patrons leave and bar goes out of business]

= = = = = = = = = = = = = = = = = =

= = = = = = = = = = = = = = = = =

[A Marketing Persona walks into a bar]
"I want an experience that fits my mood."
"Are you an Extravert Optimizer or so?"
[Orders same beer as everyone else]

= = = = = = = = = = = = = = = = =

= = = = = = = = = = = = = = = = =

[A market researcher walks into a bar]
"I'm here to find the truth"
"We're here to forget the truth"
[Writes report on Millennials instead]

= = = = = = = = = = = = = = = = =

= = = = = = = = = = = = = = = = =

[A Six Sigma Black Belt walks into a bar]
"Whatever you're doing, you're doing it all wrong."
"Fuck off"
[Everyone orders another drink & life goes on]

= = = = = = = = = = = = = = = = =

= = = = = = = = = = = = = = = = =

[An Early Adopter walks into a bar]
"You do accept Bitcoins, right?"
"No."
[Orders six-pack on Amazon Prime and drinks at home, alone]

Make It Worth The Trouble

**IF YOU WORK FOR FREE, I INVEST ZERO AND
WE LAUNCH TWO YEARS AGO...
WE MIGHT JUST MAKE ENOUGH TO HIT OUR
TARGETS.**

Make It Worth The Trouble

The theory is easy. Leverage your capabilities across the marketing mix, staying close to home for innovation designed to protect existing business, and go wild when a more disruptive impact is aspired.

Creating products that consumers love in tests is easy: just give them what they want. Creating products they love and make money for you is a different matter. Success is then defined by the degree to which you can use your current people, capabilities and assets. If you're looking to create a new product to launch next year to nudge a competing brand out of the way, then your current manufacturing assets will likely be the limiting factor. So you need to find a way to answer the consumer frustration you found, with solutions that you can make in your factory now. If you're looking to create longer term innovations to open up a new audience of consumers in another aisle in the supermarket, then your sales team's capability to build new customer relationships might well be the limiting factor you need to work within.

To succeed, one has to understand and acknowledge what the limiting factors will be to achieve success. Crudely summarized:

- For renovation and close-in innovation, your existing assets are the limiting factor; be it manufacturing, brand, channel dependence etcetera. Simply because you have neither the time, nor the likely ROI to commit to anything expensive or complicated. Create ideas accordingly.
- For more dramatic innovation aimed at attracting new consumers and drive growth, your organizational structure, capability and culture will more likely be the

constraint. But the likely returns much higher and your timeline is probably set accordingly.

The problem isn't this theory, but that many businesses either don't acknowledge their constraints, or want their cake and eat it. To some degree, this is pure optimism bias at work. But there is a darker side, which is that in many FMCG businesses the organizational structure and KPI's have been stacked against succeeding.

In many FMCG businesses, responsibility for innovation has shifted to Marketing and Consumer Insight teams. The reason of course being to get to a smarter, more consumer centric portfolio. Which is fabulous. But the possible downside is serious.

- Firstly, Marketers seldom have a background in R&D or Operations, which means they seldom truly understand how their products are made, misjudge feasible versus affordable and find out too late what really can be done at what cost. In the quick-response context of renovation, they might be lured to copying what they see competitors do, ignorant that they might be working off completely different technology. To make matters worse, with Marketing at the innovation helm, it's also in the hands of people with the fastest career churn in the business.
- With innovation responsibility and influence seeping away from R&D and Operations, their role is basically reduced cost optimization: "Just make it cheap". That mindset is corrosive, not because it's a bad but because it's addictive. An engineer will take great pride from squeezing cost out that no consumer notices.[18] And that

---

[18] Eventually, they notice. Salami slicing never goes unpunished.

mindset spreads and becomes the starting point for any request coming in, including new innovation. And in order to make something new at the best cost, you need the newest production kit. Old lines are written off too soon, and the volumes promised to cover investing in the new ones never come.

- When the relationship between the innovation defining and creation forces are disturbed as above, the business innovative capability spirals downward. Marketers push to outsourcing NPD production and lose tremendous margin, whilst manufacturing assets lie idle that could have crafted a much higher margin alternative albeit not as cheaply as current cash cows.

Effectively innovating businesses are insight-led and asset-out in their work, especially in renovation and mid-term innovation. They join up the demand and supply functions that make ideas work commercially.

Meanwhile in the domain of disruptive innovation, things have changed dramatically (no pun intended). In the mid-2010's, a new problem surfaced in many FMCG businesses: category growth plateau'd or even declined. While at the same time digital companies were growing sky high. Within a very short time span, this ignited FMCG boardroom belief that the innovation and development models used in software would unlock the same growth. Enter the Lean Start-up, the Incubator, Agile working, etcetera.

The premise was in fact very good: idea development with lots of experimentation, iteration with many prototypes. Launching and immediately improving, testing in market. It's good stuff, especially for driving breakthrough outputs. But Silicon Valley's new ways of working had a spell-binding impact on FMCG innovation functions, I suspect because the people involved would rather have work ed for a startup than a blue chip.

Five years down the line, Goliath organizations adopting David's nifty little tools have gotten themselves in a bit of trouble.

- The heralded start-ups run on different business models, with market land-grab being the main driving force objective and making a profit much less relevant. Blue chips cannot afford this.
- Many corporate incubators are sponsored entirely by a single function, e.g. Marketing. The connection to the rest of the organization is weak. When a startup does make it through to a scaleup stage, the essential support from other functions isn't there, nor rooted in shared KPI's.
- So many blue-chip incubators are working on ideas simply too small to be of interest to the mothership. Products that appear exciting and breakthrough are often quite niche. Even if they would fulfill their maximum potential in 2-3 years (say, 10's of millions revenue), they will likely still be a complete mismatch to the blue chip's requirements: 100's of millions revenue, global impact, etc. Much would be won by ruthlessly culling incubators based on true potential: only small bets, only with big potential upside.

Like with the Old Skool reality of needing to marry insight & manufacturing, the Nu Skool world has its own reality that needs acknowledging: Blue Chips are good at *scaling*, not crafting from scratch. A more successful interpretation in this reality seems to be M&A. Spot and buy the small business with the winning disruption when they're still small, adapt for mass, and then scale up.
Bingo.

Do not project onto your customers your lazy desire to keep brand & features unchanged on the premise of them wanting 'iconic' experiences.

The positioning alphabet runs from 'A' to 'THE'.

Is there AI to detect bad taste? Probably not, for it's impossible to calibrate.

Always remember that Nature has more things that can kill you than can heal you.

Hey Engineer; you could do a full Failure-Mode-And-Effects-Analysis on your design, OR you just ask my mother to panic over all its dangers.

Simplicity implies deconstruction, then reduction, to retain whatever core matters.

2010 Food innovators at work:
"Leek" – nah
"Broccoli" – nope
"Spinach" – too 1930's Popeye
"Kale" – yuck
"Onion" – makes my eyes water. Wait, go back one?

Can we agree not to refer to start-ups as 'successful' until they reach at least some kind of breakeven? Before then, the jury's still out.

Is it me, or has Tell Sell reinvented itself as the Instagram ad feed? Seriously, it's a non-stop barrage of useless crap.

MARKETING ASKS IF YOU CAN MAKE THE AROMA EXPERIENCE MORE 'EXTRAVERT' AND 'SPIRITUAL'.

What is the marketing/sales term for the following discrepancy?
- CD Players cost $250
- DVD Players that can play CD's & 20 other formats are $50

UX Designer: 'So it's better to do one click 1000 times, than 1000 clicks only once?'
Bruce Lee: 'I said kicks and that's not what I meant'

Hotel light switch designers come from the same design schools as hotel shower control designers. The design school of shit.

Once you experience that viability, not creativity is innovation's main challenge, you immediately appreciate Creators over Creatives more.

The urge to simplify all concepts to 'single benefit/minded' was driven by comms and research, not by people creating or buying products.

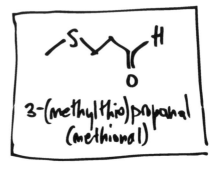

3-(methylthio)propanal
(methional)

...AND WHAT MAKES THIS REALLY EXCITING IS THAT IT SMELLS OF CAMEMBERT.

Consumer goods innovators everywhere are adopting Agile and running sprints, just like in software development. Fine, but has anyone broken them the news yet this is followed by endless rounds of debugging?

"Hey, my cousin Tony can get me a great deal on shuttle trains." – Design team meeting, planning Seattle Tacoma Airport.

There should be a Hippocratic oath for product designers, pledging not to kill their users.

Full of emotion, I typed ""(:*,') +_!!!""" and hit send. Then realized "thank you!!" with alt- instead of shift- doesn't communicate well.

It's much easier to show 'craft' by working from a low benchmark than a high one. Gourmet hamburgers vs winning a second Michelin star.

Yellow Sharpies... Why? Discuss.

'What problem are we solving here?'
#ForgottenInnovationQuestions

My new noise cancelling headphones are great for flights, they completely cancel out the applause of the tourists on board.

A start-up in "pre-revenue phase" is a hypothesis, not a business.

Is it me, or are architects very arrogant when it comes to their buildings' inhabitants suggesting other ways of using their creations?

I found email spam a lot friendlier when it was just about penis enlargements. Now it's a daily barrage of phishing scams.

Contains Ascorbic acid. EEEW
Contains Preservative. EEEW!
Contains Vitamin C. YAAAY!!
... How to push-pull with only one ingredient."

Which is the most compelling benefit; Comfort or Pain Management?

You just know a prototype test is going to be fantastic if you're given goggles, earplugs, a helmet and are then asked to stand back a bit.

True craftmanship: when there are no layers between someone's actions and the beautiful result of those actions.

"Maybe we should invent a new word to describe this new idea of ours?" – The moment a bad idea gets worse.

Stevia. My brain gets it, my taste buds don't.

Why not try LESS 'user experience' to improve your product/service, rather than more?

Movie pitch 'Food Science, The Musical'
Nutritionist discovers new superfood berries but Evil EFSA
auditor forbids claims. Fight in court, fall in love when they
realize it's only the taste that matters.
The End.

— · — · — · — · — ·

Movie pitch 'The Ladder'
Man frustrated in corporate job, barrier to promotion proves
frustrating, then discovers hierarchy is only a figure of
imagination.
The End.

— · — · — · — · — ·

Movie pitch 'The Freelancer'
Made redundant, woman makes discovery that 'Unemployed,
begging for work' and 'Liberated looking for fun work' are the
same thing.
The End.

— · — · — · — · — ·

Movie pitch 'Cash Flow Jungle'
Start-up founder fails to find seeding capital. Decides to
bootstrap, retain 100% ownership and grow organically instead,
lives happily ever after in great wealth.
The End.

Today I learned the word "Floccinaucinihilipilification", which means "the action or habit of estimating as worthless".

"Is it simply glorious?" – would be fine by me as idea selection criterium. It's also surprisingly binary: you can't have a somewhat glorious idea.

The only people more annoyingly in-my-way at airports than tourists, are tourists' extended family dropping them off or picking them up.

Over-simplified problem statements elicit over-simplified solutions.

These poor start-up founders nowadays, they're just tooo busy. Like having to go meet other start-up founders at conferences three times a week. Back in the old days we only had to focus on our clients.

I probably had a Soylent-equivalent diet during my student years, but what if I'd continued in the 25 years since?

I believe one and the same company developed the US market for cubicles and public toilets.

Try explaining a Mb/Gb data plan to anyone under 35 and you realize they were never really restricted by things like floppy disks, bandwidth, finite storage.

[Union Jack: My preferred Pritt stick pattern.]

Think of Artificial Intelligence like artificial sweeteners. Once hailed as the future of humanity but held back by the odd aftertaste.

Airline oxygen mask: "please note the bag does not inflate". FFS WHY NOT MAKE IT SUCH THAT DOES INFLATE AND NO ONE PANICS?!

'YOU'RE DOING IT ALL WRONG' – UX designers at testing labs yelling at the respondents.

New XBox console will run at 12 Teraflops, roughly level with the world's supercomputers in 2001. Somehow I had thought there would be less than19 years difference. Nevertheless, imagine the Cray team sneaking in a game of Call Of Duty while downloading the latest Janet Jackson.

I just switched on a heater in a hotel room where the air conditioning can't be switched off. I'm expecting rain & a Greenpeace raid in here soon.

Why haven't travel agencies repositioned their Single's holidays as Selfie Holidays yet? You're missing a trick here, guys.

Lack of creativity is not the reason you're not successfully innovating. It's your capability to be creative within business constraints.

A: "What kind of tech interests you?"
B: "The kind of tech that only makes a sound when I drop it."

Idea not good enough yet? Add the prefix "Natural", "3D Printed", "Gluten-Free", "IoT-Connected", "VR-Enabled" or "Graphene". Hey presto!

Two half-baked ideas do no count as one fully baked one.

Her: "You don't understand my needs!"
Him: "Just tell me what you want!?"
Her: "You should know!"
Him: "Be specific please!"
[Marketing + R&D]

Add 'gamification' to commoditized services and you'll make them more cumbersome, not more fun.

"It's the winning idea!" – Statement from someone yet to discover the difference between potential and actual impact.

Humans are primarily fear driven creatures, as a creative consequence we're much better at brainstorming for problems than we are solutions.

It seems most creativity techniques assume you need to be uncomfortable to work outside your comfort zone. How stupid.

[Most people asking for more ideas simply need fewer better ones.]

"I want more leather!" – Car interior designer who needs less plastic first.

Would the team who created Panavision Ultrawide screens appreciate that 60 years later, most videos are in Ultra Narrow Portrait format?

Good improvisation is based on experience. Which makes it more of a memory effort than a creative effort.

[Giving tour of our house]
Mouth: "And that's my son's LEGO."
Brain: "My LEGO. All mine."

Graveyard for failed bike-sharing start-ups, Hangzhou, China

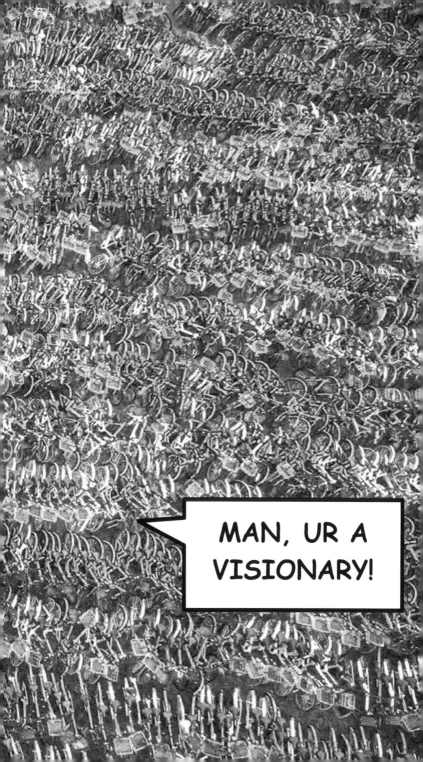

I suspect that financially successful artists find their inspiration in business books.

If you systematically manipulate concepts to pass a database driven hurdle, then you're filling your database with fabricated concepts.

Will car brands' self-driving algorithms follow their stereotypes?
Alfa Romeo: anti-social
BMW: speeding
Peugeot: at 75% of speed limit
Hummer: too close behind
Fiat: One gear too low

Is there a question imaginable where the answer is: "You need more tattoos"?

**Tinkering Excel sheets versus tinkering prototypes ...
Two worlds that seldom meet.**

If your consumers knew what % of the price they're paying is for funding the "amazing-shelf-presence" pack vs the product inside, they'd not buy it.

Storage byte sizes are 1,000's times more now than they were 25 years ago. Also the OralB® brush timing app is 76Mb, so overall no progress.

Ergonomics being taught at Industrial Design courses is a bit cynical if students end up working in passenger airplane seat design.

Just like in the movies, in innovation projects it's stunt doubles doing the heavy lifting for the movies stars who take home the prizes

160/[AGE] = Number of hours you can sleep comfortably on an inflatable camping mattress.

[Positioning: don't describe what it is, but how it's different.]

Do not overestimate what technology can accelerate or simplify. My case: e-Passport customs control.

Is there a name for the future moment that digital consumer cameras surpass the resolution of Kodak Ektachrome? Or has it already happened?

Remember: improving is one thing, inflating another.

There's a reason no one has yet invented homeopathic laundry detergent, and it's not because of the dirty laundry.

Funny how creative gurus working in innovation truly believe and insist that creativity is the only problem preventing successful innovation.

Nowadays true 'smartness' can only be judged by how well a device performs when disconnected from the internet. Same for people, by the way.

I drove a car through Naples and came out al dente.

I presented two webinars to 100 innovators and I told one half there's always a good solution, the other half there's always a good problem.

Anyone reducing people's trust in household remedies as 'superstition' isn't acknowledging what drives trust in today's modern solutions.

Disappointed there are things you simply cannot 'accelerate' or 'fast-track'? Just giving them more attention will do fine too.

Tip. Pre-heat your coffee cups with a coffee beforehand. You're welcome.

Crudely paraphrasing Robert Capa: "If your ideas aren't good enough, you're not close enough."

Fact: if you cycle through rain long enough, capillary action drives water up via your socks, trousers into your underpants. I have proof.

Hey tourist, do you wear that silly plastic poncho at home too, when it rains? Just asking.

[I think some creative agencies would do well to assign an Uncreative Director, to counterbalance some of the fluff they generate.]

If your take on innovation is chasing flavours of the day, instead of genuine progress, then you'll always remain fragile to competitors' flavour updates.

Beauty transcends the sum of parts, which is why there is often beauty where parts are missing.

Every new encounter with experienced innovators starts with exchanging war stories and showing scars. Physical scars, in particular.
"...and then that gasket that couldn't blow, did.""

[Tweeting after nice concert]
Thank you Radishes.
Fuck you Autocorrect.
Thank you Radiohead.

Sometimes a stock photo says more than a 1,000 words. But it usually just says 'stock photo'.

Again, I witness one of innovation's great miracles, an idea that sounds stupid but for peculiar reasons works: easyJet Speed Boarding.

Murphy's Law is only a problem for those who can't fix things.

Every successful new idea will have passed through multiple stages of being a bad one.

A self-driving motorcycle. Now THAT would be scary.

Hey marketers, it's good product your consumers will come back for, not more storytelling.
No product, no repeat.

Engineering, like music, reveals the fundamental beauty of ideas with a purpose.

"Stay calm, count to #FF" – a Javascript coder losing patience.

Just spoke with a client who moved from Switzerland to France, and all the hassle such transition brings. Like going from QWERTY to AZERTY.

Just a note to confirm New Jersey is the best place for consumer work on Xylitol. Because pronunciation.

Borrow with pride
– and keep your lawyer on speed dial.

"Internet of Things". Aka the belief that two commoditized, stupid devices can have a meaningful conversation.

Every touch-point on a customer journey is a touch-point too many. Journeys with less steps always win. TOUGH LUCK, UX DESIGNER.

"Is it good quality?"- Close eyes, mentally fast-forward 10 years of operation, open eyes. Still OK? Works for products, buildings & people.

Great Packaging drives trial, great Product drives repeat.

Workshops... there's always ONE person who insists on writing their post-its in portrait rather than of landscape orientation.

Billion dollar idea: Q-tips you ARE allowed to stick in your ears. FFS

Proof that owning good domain names beats trademarks is in the silly trademarks that are being registered nowadays to pair with domains.

Your product is merely an obstacle between your consumer/user and what benefit they want from the product. Fewer layers in between is always better.

Does your organization have MBA's as so-called guardians for innovation to keep the creatives in check? Show me the successes that brought.

Hey service designer. Remember your service is a means to an end, not the end itself. The less steps/clicks/calls, the better.

SEARCH(String$("Happiness");Area$(CITRIX))=FALSE

** SPOILER ALERT ** Optimizing concept copy in accordance to Quant supplier suggestions helps you beat their database, not the real market.

The difference between Design and Engineering is the level of bullshit you can get away with.

The best thing in bread since sliced bread turns out to be non-sliced bread. Go figure, Progress.

Somewhere, someone has a full-time job undoing what you do full-time for a living. Yet you both go to work every day, feeling productive.

Whatever you consider as 'packaging design' will be considered by your end consumer as UN-packaging design. You assemble, they disassemble.

Intelligence comes in shades, which goes for Artificial Intelligence too.
- Paranoid AI email filter
- Comforting AI Customer Service chatbot
- Conservative stock market AI advisor
- Reckless self-driving AI controls
- Cooking app with sweet tooth AI

I refuse to say 'OK Google' to my phone, and just tap instructions instead. Is that my introvert nature or am I just old fashioned?

'I store my stuff in the Cloud' rings differently than
'I save my files on one of Google's servers in Atlanta.'

After another 25 years of gorging on hipster burgers and cane sugar macarons, Millennials of 2040 will undoubtedly launch organic insulin shots.

'MUHAHAHA FOOLS!' – What I think every time someone offers voluntarily to have their hand luggage placed in the hull.

Character in Lord Of The Rings, Or Decorative Paint Brand?

Valspar	Jotachar	Betolux Akva
Wijzonol	Glidden	Owatrol
Finngard	Alphaxylan	Jotun Treolje
Miranol	Tikkurila	Wilcombe Cotton
Rubbol	Amphibolin	Vorlack
Haftgrund	Histolith	Hempadur

The new Marvel harder-than-diamond superhero. Part Man, Part Buckminster-Fuller Graphene.

On the increase of non-medicinal brands considering cannabis as ingredient.
1) Make propositions for multi-person consumption.
2) Include something edible like peanut butter sandwiches"

Electric car designers should look at storing energy in on-board trays of lasagna, that stuff stays frigging hot forever.

Gen-X: 'Topic_Date_Author_Version.doc, 744Kb'
Gen-Y: 'Hangry Final Final REV6.pptx, 125Mb'
Gen-Z: 'LOL.mp4, 2.4Gb'"

Does Tesla's anti-collision algorithm allow for certain exemptions? Asking for a friend.

After your concept fails in testing, should you...
A) Blame writer
B) Blame researcher
C) Blame respondents
D) Retest until it passes"

I have the impression we're shifting from an addiction to oil, to an addiction to electricity.

NOW MOVE FFS

**I UNDERSTAND IT'S READY TO GO
AND YOUR TEAM IS WAITING, BUT
LET'S RE-CUT THAT POWERPOINT A
COUPLE MORE TIMES AND GET A
FEW MORE PEOPLE TO WEIGH IN.
ALSO, WE NEED LINE OF SIGHT ON
THE Y3 VOLUME FORECAST WITH A
LITTLE MORE GRANULARITY.**
OH AND THE SALES SVP HAD A GOOD POINT, I THINK...

NOW MOVE FFS

Paralysis, inertia and utter cowardice are perhaps the most underlit reason for innovation programs grinding to a halt. The act of keep the momentum through all layers of decision-making, without letting 'risk-aversion' get in the way, is undeniably a tremendous effort. And that's not surprising, as the typical corporate innovation stage gate is designed to stop ideas from passing, rather than lovingly developing them.

I suspect a significant part of the capability to act on an innovative idea, the willingness to back it and move to action, is rooted at the very beginning of the journey. Is the business objective of the innovation understood, and has the route to creating a solution been pegged at the right level of impact. Incremental tweaks in accordance to category norms for small objectives, or bold idea shored by smart experiments and proof points for a big ambition. Both ends of the spectrum obviously carry their particular risk/reward balance, and if incorrectly matched it will surely feel like a bad idea. Especially to a decision making committee who need to decide based on hearsay, e.g. a PowerPoint presentation. If the business syntax describing risk/reward in innovation isn't clear, then amount of misunderstanding and backtracking will make every innovation project a long, long slog to work through.

It seems that in large corporate environments, there are two product launches to work through. The internal one, with a slow ramp-up of momentum, and then the real-world one. And where you want the external launch to be big and brash, you want the internal one as small and nimble as possible.

Engage internal & external stakeholders accordingly, such that they will invest in turning your ideas into reality. The impact levels make the difference. Protect-level innovation initiatives are often small improvements that can be planned by the calendar by a single team. Keep senior management far away. The other two levels, innovation for growth or disruption, need a harmonious business ecosystem to survive. Grow-level is truly opportunity-led and will require collaboration between disciplines to create new standards. Transformational innovation requires a bold vision and even bolder personality to push it through. But across all three, an energized business climate is required to keep innovative ideas intact through to the end – developing them positively, not compromising them and losing sight of the business objective that ignited the process in the first place. Create metrics for every stage gate that drive love into the ideas, and strengthening them through incremental improvement, not culling.

In this context of driving innovative ideas through a business to a successful launch, there is often mention of an entrepreneurial mindset. What appears often misunderstood is what the entrepreneur's mindset means when it comes to innovation in large organizations. Because you don't want entrepreneurs – they are wild, undomesticated and need the real world to rumble and tumble in to figure out what works. The 'intraprenurial' mindset that works in a large corporate ecosystem is different. They have the skills to look at ideas through the lens of the business structure, the framework that needs to be 'played' to go from idea to launch. Which is much more about knowing who to convince with what, than just figuring out a good product idea. They are the slightly rebellious team members and likely have no interest in being an entrepreneur outside in the wild. They love their employer and their jobs; and they are eager to stretch the current operational straitjacket into a new shape. The more dramatic the change required the more excited they get, not because they know exactly what to do, but because they know they can make it right. They exist in every organization, in every function and are the opposites of the operational excellence people. They dislike structure and love ambiguity – just what you need to figure out how to get new things done successfully.

Corporate intrapreneurs, the rebels are resourceful to the point of being Machiavellian. With the difference being they battle for the survival of the idea. They know how to engage with internal and external stakeholders such that they will invest their skin in turning a concept into reality.

oking back at the chapters before, and wondering how to end my tips & tricks about the journey to launch with a bang – I realize there isn't really one. Though perhaps there is one cliché to be brought back into the spotlight.

TRUST.

I'm typing this on August 22nd 2020. Tomorrow is my 24th anniversary of my graduation as an Industrial Design Engineer. In all those years of working in product innovation, I have never seen a team work through to a successful launch of any kind without a solid foundation of trust among them. Only *trust* allows teams to work with ambiguous criteria, with the liberty to figure things out when they (inevitably) don't always work out as planned. Trust is what moves people , and ideas to thrive. No score cards, no manifestos, no brand KPI's can ever create that drive to push ideas through, big or small.

So... No magic ingredients, It's all about good cooking.

Behind this successful product, there is the story of someone who believed in the opportunity and pushed and pushed and pushed and then should have failed except for this case study.

Moderate Coffee Consumption" is 25 cups a day right? Asking for a friend.

Reminder: REDUCING RISK ALSO REDUCES LUCK. Remember there's no success story without some luck involved.

A: 'Awesome, are you playing Tetris?!'
B: 'FU. This is my calendar weekday view. :-(

Is time damaging, or strengthening?
[Insert hockey stick curve]

Never agree to a shorter timeline without also agreeing where you're allowed to cut corners, ie quality or budget.

[**Changing ways of working shouldn't comprise merely of adding things to do. Remove at least as many.**]

I wonder if in a parallel universe where the USSR had continued to exist, with the Cold War rivalry continuing to spew technical wonders like moon landings and Concorde... would we have cracked exothermic nuclear fusion? Competition for progress is a miraculous force.

A choice between two options contains a hidden third: not choosing. Whether that's good or bad depends on the reasons for having the options.

Things that are exceptionally fast tend to also be exceptionally fragile. And exceptionally far off mark when aimed incorrectly or stopped too late."

The luckier people are, the more they'll believe it's their god-given talent.

"The market's just not ready for this yet." – Nice excuse for when you get it completely wrong.

Can we have a moment on the effect that "Highly Effective People" have on everyone else? They pretty f'ing annoying to be around.

Monitoring. Don't confuse "concern for the monitored" with "paranoia of the monitorer". Even if embedded in one and the same person.

[
A: "There is no 'I' in 'Team'."
B: "There is no 'I' in 'Blame' either."
A: "Hahaha LOL. FU."
]

Hey MBA, believe it or not, but some things don't need managing. Same for some people.

"Just pick up the f-ing phone" – what Outlook should advise you whenever you start typing yet another reply-email.

Compromise: when you can't agree.

Hey leader, are you in front of your troops or on the hill in the back?

Asking more people more questions feels like you're getting closer to a truth, until more answers start conflicting. Which IS the truth.

[WD40] = or ≠ [Repair]. Discuss.

[Customer Centricity score] = [External email volume] / [Internal email volume].

No one ever risk-reduced their way to growth.

To convince a committee, befriend the WHOLE committee. Because the purpose of a committee is that no members can/want/dare choose alone.

If the time won by delegating a task cannot be used to create additional value, then you shouldn't have delegated.

I don't think you need a fax number on your business card anymore.

It's better having a stupid system with smart people, than a smart system with stupid people. The former adapts, the latter crumbles

Realizing at the end of a phone conference, having given smart nuggets all the way to steer conversation, that you were on mute throughout.

'Micro-managing' is in the eye of the beholder.

"Gen-Y are so agile in their decision making!" – Because they're still young and their responsibilities are a fraction of the older Gen's.

Why entrepreneurs work day & night? Coz they aren't driven by the small odds of making a fortune, but by the big odds of losing a fortune.

Hey barista, I think I'm old enough to carry my coffee to the condiments counter without a lid. Trust me on this one.

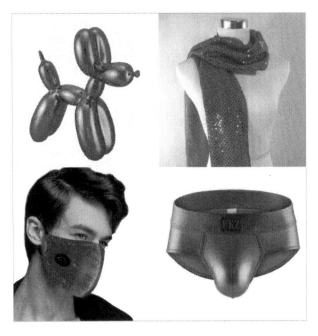

THE CIRCULAR ECONOMY BETTER HAVE SOME PATH-DEPENDANT DIRECTIONALITY, OR I'M OUT.

Planning hysteresis.
It's endlessly easier to overrun than to underrun. But that's typically not built into plans.

The only (and truly only) situation you need a perfect start, is when you won't be able to course correct. And that's almost never the case.

Risk: you can form an opinion about it, but you can't measure it. Unless it's not your own risk, then measuring is easy.

"First time right" only matters if you can make it on time too.

What do you call the opposite of "the gift that keeps on giving"?

Benefits & Risks do not sit in the same dimensions, as some kind of zero sum, balanced act. Both should be weighed and treated separately.

You cannot disrupt a market without disrupting your own organization.

Measures to reduce Risk will also reduce Luck, as the unexpected can't be classified before it presents itself.

My new concept timeline: "Preferably Yesterday", "ASAP" and "Narnia".

Planning a business war-game? Look up on LinkedIn the actual people in key roles at your competitors. More personal & insightful than SWOTs.

Being overly positive or negative about a process is quite pointless if you haven't yet agreed a destination, or even a direction.

Popular press gets excited about "Life Possible On Proximus Centauri B", skipping the fact we haven't even (dis)proven life on Mars yet.

You can have excellent overview from close by.
It's just an overview of fewer, smaller things.

The word 'Innovation' is mostly used to describe with hindsight what someone has already done, and done successfully enough to get noticed.

Opportunities come and go? Nonsense. Missed opportunities will haunt you forever.

Strategic U-turns, aka pivots... Don't just bounce from left to right and black to white without considering the middle. Lots of greys in between.

TQM Equivalent of a Gordian knot: try explaining heuristics to a Six Sigma Black Belt. To get moving, you just cut the Black Belt in half.

Preparing for a sales meeting? All you need to bring are one or two good metaphors. Seriously, that's all you need.

Pass stuff up to the echelon of decision makers & they'll do exactly that: make a decision. So pass up only when you are sure a decision is needed.

Hey entrepreneur: hire people so good you that would fire yourself if you had been in their role.

Every day is groundcoffee day.

Too few corporate hotshots have a section on their CV that records "things I made".

Straight to the periphery of the problem.

Feeling your back against the wall? An illusion because the wall is probably moving your way and pushing you.

Flying out of Brazil, CWB Gate 2. That place that mysteriously always smells of cheese.

Are you receiving challenges, or creating them?

Are your customer acquisition manager and customer retention manager still working from separate offices?

Urgent? How urgent? "Annoyed-urgent", "Sweating-urgent" or "Peeing-in-pants-urgent"?

"OMG It's *sooo* busy and we are so behind on schedule!! Let's discuss what to do after we get back from holiday in 6 weeks" – Your colleagues.

Detail-focused or detail-distracted?

Personal growth feeds business growth and vice versa. But business contraction also feeds personal growth.

Business empires crumble from risk-aversity, losing their willingness to embrace change. Make that any empire.

"As Seen On TV!" – remember that was considered a good enough reason to buy?

Real innovation requires changing the angle of decision making from "stop unless" into "let pass unless", as you have no clear benchmark.

Distract the naysayers with red herrings like neuro-MR and big data, while you get the real work done.

I THINK MY HAMBURG HOTEL ELEVATOR IS WARNING ME ABOUT TAXI APP STOCK.

Right now, a colleague of yours is thinking of all the things you should do better too.

Are you paddling or sailing?

New in the #superhero line-up: The Incredible Innovation Man... jumps to conclusions faster than a speeding bullet.

The title slide of your presentation says more than a thousand words. So, skip the thousand words and move to slide 2, please.

> **Most of what you lack in influence, you can make up with persuasion. And vice versa.**

Better to include 50% extra time for mistakes and start immediately, than wasting 50% extra time planning up front and presume no mistakes.

Ideas put on +2 year horizon "for technical reasons" are only that far out for lack of willpower. Almost anything is technically possible within 2 years.

> **Think twice, and then again, before telling someone they don't know what they're doing.**

Beware of the planner who promises running at optimal capacity.

Translating every decision into a financial one is merely a mental trick to help you feel morally exempt from the effects of that decision.

Ask yourself – what's the best metaphor to describe my job?

When gambling, gamble some chickens and maybe a goat. Never the whole ranch and certainly not your spouse. #Metaphor

"We need more examples" – always, regardless of how many examples you provide.

French in-flight announcements in English are the audio equivalent of a doctor's scribble on a prescription. Important but incomprehensible.

Long ago, people thought you'd fall off At World's End. I still think that at AMS H7.

"Wait a minute... maybe I'M the problem myself!?" – only enlightened people.

> **Courage: put your intuition out in the open for scrutiny, ahead of the facts coming in.**

Risk averse mind-set: delusion all options can be known before starting. Innovation success originates in one's confidence to course correct.

"10 Tips to harness your business growth" – As if today's businesses need constraints on their unsustainable, life-threatening growth.

"The first thing we're doing to get out of this mess my predecessor left, is create a new logo." – New CEO's.

The fundamental difference between fast/cheap innovation programmes and long/expensive ones is the amount of risk/ambiguity one's accepting.

"No Action" is often the better option, but less understood by stakeholders and impossible to take credit for.

What you struggle to understand, trying to explain it will just take you further away. Let your subconscious play with it for a few days.

CPG/FMCG Innovation teams tend to overlook there's really only one party they need to convince: the retailer selling their stuff.

You can't instruct someone to be more entrepreneurial. At best, you can remove restraints that weren't self-imposed.

Be brave and work towards an ambitious new comfort zone. 'Design Thinking' anagrams to 'Thin Skinned Gig'

Suggested names for the ratio between 'energy spent debating an idea' versus 'energy it would take to pilot the idea' on a spectrum from 0<1 & 1<∞.
- The Inertia Threshold
- The Tinkerer's Razor
- The Inventor's Facepalm
- Chatterbox over Sandbox score
- Tittle-tattle to go-to-battle index
- Elbowing to elbow grease
- Slagging over slogging gap
- The Worrier/Warrior Scale

Failure, Defeat and Ruin – three very different things, but often raked onto one pile by risk analysts and inspirational quote writers.

I ran GVA Security to D75 in under four minutes. I'm sure that's worth some kind of formal accreditation?

Work experience stages
1) I want to join the machine
2) Help I'm a cog in the machine
3) Fight the machine
4) OMG There is no machine

PRO-TIP FOR VIDEO CONFERENCING PRANKS: WEAR A MOIRÉ-EFFECT INDUCING STRIPED SHIRT TO ANNOY EVERYONE INSTANTLY.

Disruptive Start-ups are a little bit like tempestuous teenagers, they need to go out and try their wild stuff... and find for themselves that not all of the old ways were bad. Progress is about breaking ties with the past selectively, rather than totally.

[Excuses for unprofitable activity]
"We always do it this way!"
"It's strategic!"
"The other thing was even worse!"
"Need to do SOMEthing!"

When embarking on a journey, "I got your back" is worth infinitely more than "Good luck"

Occam's Razor redux: never attribute to talent what can adequately be described as luck.

Can one have multiple Comfort Zones?

'BE QUIET, DON'T EVEN BREATHE' What I think while I struggle to find the 'disconnect' button after the goodbyes at the end of a conference call.

Every product category has a metaphorical equivalent to 'weeds'.

Open Innovation is difficult, because large companies are set up to buy raw materials, services and other companies. Not for buying ideas.

I wonder if Apple Inc would have been as successful if the Steves had given it a modern day, misspelled, stupid name like Appl, APPEL, Aqqle, …

I suspect the majority of feuds between Marketing and R&D teams originated when one team said "feasible" and the other heard "affordable".

I've only seen a fraction of the poorly used iceberg metaphors in business presentations.

Pro travel tip: when without travel adapter, use the USB port on the back of your hotel room TV to charge your phone

'We need to communicate better' is often actioned as 'We need to send more emails'

Many organizations understand the importance of systematic removal of cost but forget the equivalent importance of systematic addition of value.

Short business books should be more expensive than long ones. If they're written from experience, that is.

"Glacial" is a speed.
And "backwards" is a direction.
LOOK AT THE BRIGHT SIDE OF THINGS

Ensure to take care not to double up on additional pleonasms in your PowerPoint presentation slides.

I suspect a good way to break into a building is to come dressed as an alarm maintenance person.

[**The anvil is in the detail.**]

'Am I willing to work through weekends to make this thing work?' #ForgottenInnovationQuestions

An exceptionally safe place to store passwords nowadays, is a 5.25" floppy disk. Guaranteed unreadable except by the most expert of experts.

Skunkwork projects running 'below radar' in your business reveal the remarkable truth that in reality, difficulties come from within rather than outside.

Maybe we just blockchain some of these blockchain experts, for some peace & quiet?

Excellence is a moving target – everywhere except in ISO process manuals.

It strikes me as quite desperate how non-US retailers across the globe have copied 'Black Friday Sales' after a perfectly normal Thursday.

What makes you more "tourist"?
1) Repacking your luggage at check-in counter.
2) Debating 300ml shampoo bottle with scanner operator

Kodak, Nokia, Polaroid – Juicy stories where large companies lost out to changing times. BUT they are anomalies. The big players almost always win.

Every time you say Millennial, a Baby Boomer dies.
[Paraphrasing Mr Rikki Marr]

Let's be honest. 50 years of pushing the food pyramid as healthy diet has left half the global population with love handles. Often significant, flabby love handles.

[Discomfort strengthens.]

"I'm SO busy!" – worst last words.

I see on TikTok that Gen-Z has discovered the fun of Mentos® & Coke®.

Post-its don't kill workshops. Pointless creative exercises kill workshops.

Maybe you could 3D print yourself out of trouble?

Don't see everything you believe.

You don't want a cheap tattoo. Or a hasty doctor. Carry that mentality across into other parts of your life, it'll be better for it.

Disruptive innovation requires disruptive people. Aka the kind that corporate environments tend to neutralize with KPI's.

Bought a Fitbit. Now considering cheats.

If you're regularly out of stock – do you have a distribution problem, or a pricing problem?

Is it me, or are dual presentations on conference stages (as in, two people together) almost always confusing? It's seldom done for the benefit of the audience.

Not seen any over-excited tweets about Hyperloop in my feed for a while. Anyone still working on that?

Free upgrades to business class still make me squeal like a teenage tourist.

'Disruptive Innovation' anagrams to
- 'Avid Intuitions, Proven'
- 'Intuitive Non-Pro Divas'
- 'Purist, Avoid Invention'"

'Launch' isn't a moment or phase transition, but a period of time. Quite a long one actually.

The worst thing you can do to an insecure decision maker: feed them even more good alternatives.

"Roughly right" beats "Precisely wrong", always.

It's probably wise to scrap all ambitions for disruptive innovation if your procurement team can't register new suppliers in less than 6 months.

Hotel alarm clocks: the least trusted devices on earth.

Every success story I know involves some degree of plain luck. Therefor do keep some of your work unplanned, simply to stumble on something good you hadn't expected.

"He has visionary ideas, just not very realistic" – in other words, quite useless.

If you're not the type to procrastinate, you can choose to over-intellectualize instead.

MS Project – meant for planning projects but instead used for recording what actually happened.

[Looks at clock for mercy]
[None granted, as usual]

Hey retailers, I'm pretty sure Monday can't count as Black Friday anymore. Hold yourself together please.

'B' and 'E' – the inflight seating equivalent of drawing the short straw.

Interpreting Parkinson's Law. Don't complain about the pointless reporting you do, unless you can show what you'd rather do with time instead.

Your faith in statistical confidence correlates directly with the amount of your own money sunk in the implications of acting upon it.

Happy-anger, aka WTF-anger, can be a very powerful and positive creative force.

The value is remembered long after the price is forgotten.

Risk is less perceived in context of potential reward, and more in perspective of potential ruin.

Epilogue: When The World Falls Apart

I'LL PASS THIS PROJECT ON TO
YOUR SUCCESSOR, NEXT YEAR OR SO.
CAN YOU CREATE A HANDOVER DECK?
BTW YOU KNOW YOU'RE FIRED, RIGHT?

Epilogue: When The World Falls Apart

I'm compiling this 3rd Grumpy Innovator book three months into the 2020 Corona crisis and a market meltdown. That's pretty tough if you're running a small business. And the outlook is worrying, to say the least. What now? If you're reading this after everything has returned to prosperity, well done on surviving! If the pandemic is still raging, read on.

For what it's worth, a few thoughts for owners and entrepreneurs of small businesses, especially the young ones. At Happen we were just over a year old when we went through a similar global economic collapse in 2008 when Lehman Brothers fell.

Daily business seemed to evaporate overnight. Everything changed, just like it 2020 is proving to do. Back then, we survived and eventually thrived. Plenty of luck and good business friends obviously, but what else?

First and foremost: **be aware you have control**. As a small, self-owned business, you can respond much quicker (and in your own favour) better than you ever could as a large business. That said, if you're over your eyeballs in VC then it's someone else's money at stake and you might as well walk away now. Screw 'em and start over. Or make an offer to buy back your business for peanuts, in full. You know your business better than they do.

Throw your old business plan out the window, if you even had one to start with. Its assumptions will prove mostly nostalgic, even laughable a few years from now.

The paranoid survive. By that I do not mean that taking risks or changing track is bad, on the contrary. But you can only go bust once and the threshold for going bust will now be much lower.

The market will get much worse before it gets better because second-order effects still need to kick in. In fact this time it is worse to start with, given Corona prevents people interacting normally outside of the financial markets. Things will not return to the old state, the new normal will be different when it settles down 2-3 years from now. Which might be a longer waiting period than you've even been in business for.

Your client portfolio will need to change quickly, as all of them will be going through frantic change themselves now. Your current largest client might disappear, a tiny one might become huge. As long as you're willing to change quickly yourself.

Business development before delivery. This should actually always be the case if you intend to grow, but it's even more true now. Do you have a team who can convince clients to continue to work with you? Are they just mouths to feed, or are they feeding you back? Take a hard, honest look.

Immerse in the debt situation of your clients, and the fragility of the industry they are in. Then be brutal in your choice which ones to stay away from, or ask up-front payment from. Your pockets probably aren't very deep. So your time and resource is better spent on finding new clients that represent the new normal, than potentially losing everything on a fragile client taking your revenue down with them.

Adapt your offer to what matters in the new world, to keep your clients' projects moving. Prevent stalling, your clients will love you for being nimble. For us, the main new innovation methodologies we developed in those days were

'Sweating Assets', i.e. innovate asset-out from the factory to guarantee 'zero CapEx required' for your innovation. Also, it triggered us to develop online research tools (radical in 2008) which led to the birth of our Winkle team in 2009; now Happen Research & Analytics.

Cash is King... hold on to it, EVERY PENNY. Spread it across multiple banks, as even banks can topple. Any expense not serving your primary purpose is an expense wasted. Also "Leaders eat last", as per ancient adagium. Your own salary can wait, as that's also cost to the business: one that you can choose to raise again in better times.

Know your 'uncle point' and act on it. Instead of trying to predict how things will unfold (no one can) make 100% clear to yourself what your worst acceptable situation is, the rock-bottom at which you pull the kill switch. This might be ahead of a next round of monthly payments. This is important because entrepreneurial optimism might drag you deeper into trouble than you can afford.

Pay your suppliers on time, all of them. As a small business, your survival might be dependent on them as much as vice versa. Also, you probably know them personally, and they know your business and category deeply. They are the best sounding board for evolving your business into the new reality.

Prepare for longer payment terms to become standard. Back in 2008, most of our clients went up from 30 to 60 or even 90 days and have stayed there since. I wouldn't be surprised to see that go up to 90 and 120 across the board. Organize your business to be able to deal with this and keep the clients who do pay faster close to your heart with extra service. Equally, be merciless in chasing outstanding invoices. Hiring someone to chase them for you will free you up to hunt new business.

Remember that as owner you are in control and surrounded by entrepreneurial employees who enjoy the hustle of being in a small business. A team who will be more willing to change track and try new things with you than you might think!

In the meantime, stay safe and prosper.

Democracy is on a slippery slope when/where people approach it as a consumer right rather than a civilian duty.

Entropy always wins. Life is literally about fighting it to the death.

Dutch proverb: "If you burn your ass, you must sit on the blisters". Relevant stuff, those Dutch proverbs.

An MBA might get your career unstuck, but not your life. You need other things for that.

"Shaken, not stirred" – James Bond describing how his first project debrief made him feel.

Reality = Actual facts
Observation = Perceived facts
Story = Interpreted facts
BS = Created facts
Profile = Selective facts
Evidence = Any"

When looking back at hectic periods of your life, ask not HOW you coped, but WHY you coped. Much more interesting.

Is the system corrupted or has the corruption become systematic?

Did you know "Professional Lobbyist" anagrams to "Booby Trap Of Silliness".

To all politicians. Before opening your mouth, ask yourself "Would my mother approve of what I'm about to say?". Thank you.

We preach to the converted because it's easier.

Contrary to popular belief, a vegan diet of muesli burgers, organic carrot cake, soy Frappuccino® & organic beer still makes you fat.

Hypothesis: Western societal cohesion began fragmenting & drifting apart when military service was ended mid 90's and adolescents mixed less.

Fraud types:
A: Nincompoop who tumbles into it and can't stop.
B: Ruthless, manipulating opportunist.
Note: A is an illusion created by B.

"I don't get it. My presentation is clear, concise, I even do a bit of theatre. BUT NO ONE EVEN LOOKS UP." – Air hostess safety instruction.

We call it 'GMO' because 'selective inbreeding' doesn't sound nice, right?

Yes clickbait, we get it now.

When you realize that you still have over half a bag of disgusting coffee beans to grind through before you can switch back to a brand you like.

When the only power socket at the whole airport is next to the toilets' entrance. Feeling like a real junkie.

Why fool others when it's so much easier just to fool yourself?

A: "Is it walking distance?"
B: "About 20 minutes."
A: "So no."
Why humanity will not live to be 100.

Hey startup, work/think in earn-rates, not burn-rates. Seriously.

Cynics say the world runs on PowerPoint. But we all know that isn't true. It runs on Excel.

Isn't it ironic how businesses big enough to have a 'scenario planning team' are too big to adapt in time for any of their scenarios?

Anyone complaining that technocrats are running government too much like a business is giving too much credit to how most businesses are run

I don't know anyone who got fired for trying something new. But know a couple struggling to get hired for never having tried.

Sadly, many people consider their body no more than a vessel that carries their head around from A to B. Or worse, only their eyes & mouth.

I saw a DeLorean drive through The Hague this evening, which must be a happy omen of some kind.

"Live like there's no tomorrow!"
aka "Hopelessly stuck in yesterday."

Be patient, time flies anyway.

Fundamentalists and Atheists both never give serendipity the credit it deserves, mistaking it either for divine intervention or skill.

"Wow, someone actually bought something." – Air hostess after a duty-free round through the aisle, when someone actually bought something.

"Haha LOL, look at Greece struggling with their debt of 2x GDP" – Says person with a mortgage 6x their annual income.

Is the love-hate relationship politicians have with their voters comparable to marketers and their consumers? Just a hunch.

It's easier to care than to pretend to care.

The Titanic: everyone was so preoccupied with the lack of lifeboats, no one considered the iceberg as a fine place to wait for a few hours.

Merci bacon, Auto-correcte.

"And don't make any mistakes, OK?" – Useless advice given 1000's of times every day.

Access = Power

Dutch proverb: "When you're being shaven, sit very still". Relevant stuff, those Dutch proverbs.

Pre-industrial ages: Stone, Bronze & Iron.
Post-industrial ages: Stoned, Bronzed and Ironed.

Clearly demonstrated by the VW Diesel Swindle is what happens when regulators know less of the topic than the regulated. Think IT, Pharma...

Who cares about late departures? It's late arrivals that are the annoyance.

The Herd works in mysterious ways.

When you're desperate for good news, n=1 is suddenly good enough.

Western democracy went kaputt when politicians started acting as marketers to consumers of civil services – and citizens acted accordingly.

"Passengers with small children board first" – which doesn't apply to "Passengers squealing like small children".

Inserting more energy into a system, be it human/machine/environment doesn't increase its power, but its volatility.

Doing in-flight yoga poses in your airplane seat makes you look like a jerk. Or whatever the feminine word for of jerk is.

The current era of central banking policies will be known as "The Homeopathy Decade", when infinitely small rates were thought to heal.

Millennials say "Whoop!" too often.

> "If you don't like our train service, then go take a train somewhere else."
> – Service logic of train companies.

My worry isn't about more robots becoming smarter than humans. My worry is about more humans becoming dumber than robots.

When you suspect the system is corrupted, corruption probably is the system.

Politicians zoom in on the differences, diplomats on the commonalities. Which is why politicians should stay away from negotiations.

To all you nitpickers out there: have a ncie weeknd!

If the Internet were a country, it would be a pretty horrible place to live. A surveillance state full of thieves and con artists. Oh wait.

Landed at London Luton airport, which isn't in London. On to Luton Parkway station, in a bus. And the station isn't in Luton either.

This place is a web of lies.

[
I bet that of every $1 generated by digital start-ups, $3 is spent on hyping the stock.
]

Trade shrinks the differences between two countries, Politics increases them. Trade builds bridges, Politics burn them.

Evaluating my Generation-X heritage...
Ambition: Fight Club
Reality: Jackass
Legacy: Gluten-free

Trade accelerates mutual interests, interdependencies and personal conversation between people who would otherwise be strangers.

The world would be a much better place if we all took more naps. Proper, middle-of-the-day siestas.

When it comes to stimulating trade, governments can only place or remove restrictions. Via Negativa.

After 12 years of frequent flying, the one thing I've still not perfected is my disembark-to-bus technique. I always end at Customs last.

Sadly, being more opinionated is too often interpreted as being better informed.

Don't moan about today's price of cigarettes if you're happy to spend $5 on a single latte.

The quality of institutions isn't defined by the quality of their leader, but by its resilience to unqualified idiots leading it off course.

If airlines truly understood frequent flyers, the reward tiers wouldn't be Bronze-Silver-Gold but OMG-MEH-FML.

You can recognize a first world economy by the amount of money spent on fighting boredom.

History: a long string of events that prove people wrong, who thought they were right at the time.

Empathy: acceptance the other side simply doesn't know they're wrong yet.

Friday afternoon, an easyJet flight from Luton to Amsterdam. Smells of anticipation, shored up by cheap deodorant.

A: "Describe yourself in one word."
B: "Mildly rebellious."

Rank the quality of any country's institutions by whether the move people, or money upwards through the system.

In the grand scheme of things, 'grand' is probably giving today's schemes too much credit.

Antiquity. More or less the same as today, but without the penicillin, electricity and plastic.

So far, I find Brexit an anticlimax of Y2K proportions.

Business traveler truth: all beaten-up 767's end up servicing routes to Heathrow.

When will the homeopaths weigh in on #COVID19? You'd think this is their moment to shine, no?

I doubt I will recognize any April Fools' pranks today as being jokes.

Obviously once the lockdown is lifted, we'll see a dramatic rise in divorces filed ... with the dark twist that now both parties will ask for the other partner to keep the damn kids.

Right now would be a good time to prove existence of life on another planet, to put today's agitations in some well-needed perspective.

Reviving a 100 million year old microbe isnt very different from fast-forwarding the genetic code by 100 million years, aka GMO. The organism and environment haven't evolved in parallel.

Paraphrasing a friend of mine, long ago: "If you can make it to 50 without 'growing up' then your environment will absolve you of that expectation". I was too young at the time to understand that was a good thing.

Anyone complaining that members of the European Parliament lead too lavish lifestyles should come check out Strasbourg Airport. What a dump.

Shock a woke Millennial by explaining people in wheelchairs can be assholes too.

Watching 'Die Hard 2', appalled by 1990's lack of airport security.

As humans, we're horrible at distinguishing permanent versus temporary, and vice versa.

Airports without power plugs deserve to have their vending machines unplugged so I can charge my phone. I'm talking to you, Milan Linate.

The virtue of "tolerance" is mostly a well disguised "indifference", which isn't very virtuous at all.

Broadsheet news headlines containing the words "could", "might" and "expected to" are mostly not much better than fake news and buzzfeeds.

Only in New York... it's half past seven in the morning and I've already spent $12 on coffee.

Is it me, or is the Moral High Ground getting really crowded?

Big ideas can pull people, communities or even a whole nation together. Or drive them apart.

If an alien landed, commanding 'Take Me To Your Leader' ...
you can imagine the confusion that would give nowadays.

**JULY 4TH IS THE ANNIVERSARY OF THE PASSING
OF THESE TWO LOVELY HUMANS.
BE LIKE BOB. BE LIKE BARRY.
THE WORLD WILL BE A LITTLE BETTER FOR IT.**

If your public persona is slick & polished, the only way to
gain street cred seems to be a complete public unravelling,
breakdown, followed by a miraculous upswing.

Nothing says 'Monday Morning' like a Citrix logon
experience.

After Boomers, GenX, Millennials and GenZ, 2021 will give
us The Coronials. Born out of bored parents working from
home for a couple of months.

From personal experience in 2008. Big & small businesses
will indeed implode in coming months. And then LOTS of
new small businesses will be created in next 1-2 years, some
of which grow into the next generation of big ones.

It's much easier to form an objective opinion when you're
not fully informed. The more info, the more subjective is
your interpretation.

Airport perfume counters have become dystopian IKEA labyrinths. I'm talking to you, Gatwick Airport South Terminal.

Paraphrasing what I remember someone saying in the early 2000's about the fall of the Soviet Union: "Bookstores used to sell only Politburo-approved literature and Solzhenitsyn would be impossible to find. Now bookstores can sell anything they want, but only stock Stephen King."

"But my camera is on?!" – poor guy in a Zoom call who happens to have a very round face and eyes that look like his initials.

Young people who are still yapping "Covid won't kill you if you're under 60" clearly haven't thought through what "almost dying" implies.

At current innovation ambition levels, we'll end this century as we did the last one, just with Facebook and worse weather. PROGRESS PLEASE.

Baby Boomers are the first human generation to grow into adulthood without siblings dying young, thanks to penicillin. Many of them felt immortal, trusting medicine with carry them into old age. Then #COVID19 knocked on their door, to settle old debts from a life lived poorly.

What economists call growth is like saying "I jumped up in the air" without adding "and into a manhole"

I think there's a correlation between the flight seat row where the Business/Economy split screen is pegged, and the Dow Jones index.

I believe charities should have an explicit, statutory purpose of making themselves obsolete after resolving the problem they were created for.

The spectrum of life in COVID lockdown;
Elderly: life as usual
Couples with no kids: life's good
Couples with young kids: kill me
Couples with older kids: this ain't a hotel dammit
Singles: OMG booooored f**k this celibacy

If your ego drives you to calling yourself 'CEO' of small start-up, then I think 'Secretary General' is more appropriate.

What have you taken for granted recently?

I guess the Burglary industry is now switching from Consumer to Professional, with the lockdown making their work in our homes impossible.

OMG I am now 4 years older than Danny Glover was in the first Lethal Weapon went he kept saying he was too old for this shit.

I remember simpler days, when it was just Rage Against The Answering Machine.

Kind of funny to be reminded that The Kilogram is an agreement, not a thing.

Across the world, parents now working from home are having to explain their kids "yes this is what I do all day".

Your revenues might be down in these daunting times, but imagine the world emerging from lockdown and finding that nobody missed your products? Seek being relevant to your customers before anything else.

Working from home I get a lot done, but I sit so still my Fitbit thinks I died.

I love how breweries and distilleries are making sanitizer gels and giving them away for free. To keep the good vibes flowing, I have asked some of our clients who make sanitizers to switch to beer and spirits and give them away for free too.

I guess 'anti-fragility' is life's way of dealing with 'entropy' and coming out on top.

Sadly, very [narrow + polarized] messages are parading as clarity.

One full lap completed. By 'lap' I mean a full orbit around the Sun.

Gents, taking phone calls while standing at a urinal is just wrong – on so many levels.

Glossary of Innovation ~~Bullshit Bingo~~ *terms*

I'M NOT FEELING ANY PURPOSE ALIGNED WITH OUR ESSENCE HERE. CAN YOU PRETOTYPE A FEW MORE MVP'S FOR CO-CREATION?

Glossary of Innovation ~~Bullshit Bingo~~ *terms*

Normal People	Innovation People

3Y Plan

θriːʏɪər plæn – noun

A plan covering the next three calendar years.

We bought the royal mansion and made a 3Y plan for restoring it to its former glory.

A 1Y plan, made to celebrate highlights from the past year and project them onto the next. Re-written every year from scratch, to align objectives to new bonus targets.

I was challenged on my 3Y plan not delivering the desired growth, so I upped Y2 and Y3 for my successor.

360° View

θriːsɪkstivjuː - noun

A 'full circle' approach or view into a situation.

We enjoyed a 360° view of our surroundings, and could see for miles and miles into the distance.

Tends to imply an approach involving 2 to 10 parties, with the objective, perspective and outcomes optimised to the person sitting at the centre of that 360-degree panorama.

For [product] to make any profit, we'll need a 360 approach to saving cost.
Designer vantage: squeeze R&D, Manufacturing and Procurement
Procurement vantage: squeeze Manufacturing, Suppliers, expedition

---

2025 Vision

twɛn ti twɛn ti faɪvˈvɪʒ ən – noun

A view on the year 2025.

We imagine buying a house in 2025.

A chance to re-state all ambitions originally set for 2020 but trashed by the Covid crisis and naive forecasting. Given it's comfortably 4½ years out, also a chance to up the game a bit.

The cupholder brand's CMO pictured a 2025 vision of a hot beverage on the handlebars of every self-steering motorbike in the world. Bold!

Accelerator

əkˈsɛləreɪtɔr - noun

Lever connected to energy source in vehicle drive train. For example, the right foot pedal in car.

Stamping hard on the accelerator is referred to as "Pedal To The Metal".

An organisation that provides small amounts of cash, coaching and office space to a large number of start-ups named after popular nouns but with missing vowels. A numbers game, the objective being to get some of them to survive past a second investment round, so the shares can be sold on to the next sucker at profit.

The Accelerator housed 25 start-ups, 24 of which failed. But the sale of their stock in "Bleedr" made them enough return to fund another 50.

Normal People	Innovation People

Adjacency

əˈdʒeɪ sən si - noun

An area right next to where you are.

Pete stood next to me, making him an adjacency to me.

A product, occasion or opportunity that is just outside one's typical playing field. The benefit of working on finding a good adjacency is the potential to leverage technology and other business assets in a 'Blue Ocean' of opportunity, not having to build it from scratch. Comes with the bonus of a fresh set of competitors.

Dentures for cats.
Spotify for 40+ year olds.
Chocolate for men.

Agile

adʒʌɪl - adjective

Able to move quickly and easily.

Ruth hopped from queue to queue, agile as a little monkey.

A development and project planning methodology drawn from software development, transplanted to every other category under the sun. Often misunderstood because it has such a nice name.

Assemble a scrum team and get to work. See you next week, I want the outputs of sprint 1 on my desk at 08h30, thanks.

Alignment

əˈlʌɪnm(ə)nt - noun

Arrangement in a straight line or in correct relative positions.

The tiles had slipped out of alignment.

To agree something amongst a number of stakeholders. Often mistaken for talking about project status and filling the Outlook slot.

Can we align where you got to with that brief? Please ping me a Teams invite.

Archetypes

ɑːkɪtʌɪp - noun

A very typical example of a certain person or thing.

He was the archetype of the old-skool advertising man.

Simplification of consumer behaviour in the form of cliché personalities, aka personas. Often trademarked by research agencies and re-skinned for different clients and given stupid names.

"It was only when I moved to from Dairy to Detergents, that I realised Helga The Hunter-Gatherer and Elsa The Optimist Extravert were the same persona"

Normal People	Innovation People

Asset-Out

aset'aʊt - adjective

Methodology that implies working within the constraints of existing assets, mostly referring to manufacturing lines. Not to be mistaken with 'Assed-Out'.

These pet snacks were developed asset-out from the pet food lines, saving a lot of time and CapEx.

This is how every small business innovates, which is to start from existing capabilities. In larger organisations, where innovation teams, R&D, marketing and manufacturing might all sit in different countries or even continents, it's easy to lose sight of what is actually feasible and pragmatic.

When there's no money left to invest in new factory lines, make something asset-out on the old lines to keep going.

Augmented Reality

ɔːɡˈmɛntɪdˈrɪˈalɪtl - noun

A technology that superimposes a computer-generated image on a user's view of the real world, thus providing a composite view.

Every tech company under the sun is trying to find a sensible purpose for Augmented Reality.

A persistent belief that everything one can peer at through a camera lens will become a magical experience by layering additional information on top. Very few examples outside of professional applications have proven viable, or technically stable enough to last.

Point your phone's camera at café in front of you and read information provided that it's a café.

Axplore

ækˈsplɔr- verb

No equivalent in regular human language

Formally known as 'blamestorming', but more action oriented. Travel through an (unfamiliar) area in order to find out who's fault it is.

"He axplored the team & fired Henry"

Behavioral Change

bɪˈheɪvjər(ə)lˈtʃeɪn(d)ʒ - noun

A change of routine, usually after an intervention or dramatic event.

The mere sight of the cattle prod is enough to elicit behaviour change from even the most stubborn of toddlers.

Usually refers to habit change rather than behaviour change. A prime purpose in life for many marketers is to claim they have 'achieved a behaviour change' amongst their brand's consumers by switching them to a new habit that involves increased consumption of their product.

Dentures for cats.
Spotify for 40+ year olds.
Chocolate for men.

Normal People	Innovation People

Blue Ocean

bluˈoʊ ʃən - noun

Definition of a market opportunity, based on disrupting a market adjacent to one's own. Usually a market that can be simplified and democratized. Read the book by INSEAD professors W. Chan Kim and Renée Mauborgn.

Stelios spotted the Blue Ocean of no-frills air travel, founded easyJet® and gave British Airways lots of pain.

A product, occasion or opportunity that is just outside one's typical playing field. The benefit of working on finding a good Blue Ocean is the potential to leverage technology and other business assets on an adjacent opportunity, not having to build it from scratch. Comes with the bonus of a fresh set of competitors.

Our ocean is turning too Red for comfort. Find me a nice and empty Blue one please.

Big Data

bɪgˈdeɪtə - noun

Extremely large datasets that may be analysed computationally to reveal patterns, trends, and associations, especially relating to human behaviour.

Much IT investment is being done in acquiring, managing and maintaining Big Data.

In an increasingly digital world, data is being generated by almost every human interaction imaginable. This data is collected in 'lakes' for analysis and spotting useful patterns.

"I NEED MOAR DATA"

Burn Rate

bəːn reɪt - noun

The speed at which a fire, flame or glow consumes a fuel such as coal or wood.

A fire burned and crackled cheerfully in the grate, we knew we'd be comfortable for the evening.

Speed at which an organisation is spending its investors' money.
Not to be confused with entrepreneurship, which involves spending one's own money.

They're buying companies like they're swiping through f-ing Tinder®. At this burn rate they'll be dead by Xmas.

Normal People	Innovation People

Burning platform

ˈbɜr nɪŋ ˈplæt fɔrm - noun

A raised construction that has been set alight.

The Brighton Pier for a few hours in May 2003.

A topic of paramount importance to the business, or at least the CEO, for the survival of the business.

Snack food CEO's have made "healthy snacking" a burning platform, to keep regulators from intervening.

Cat man

kæt mæn - noun

Male cartoon character of mixed human/feline form.

Batman's nemesis Cat Man struck again.

Category Manager, carrying responsibility over a defined part of the product/service portfolio of an organisation. Often referring to a subset that has no equivalent outside of the organisation amongst customers or consumers.

Since my promotion to Cat Man, I look after our P&L for Juicy Crackers.

Circular Economy

ˈsɜr kyə lər ɪˈkɒn ə mi - noun

A closed economy of goods, with no depletion of (natural) resources.

We sort and recycle different plastic waste products to convert into virgin material for the packaging industry.

A particular spin on Sustainability principles, that drives for closed circle (flow) of materials. Waste is minimised and after the usable life of a product, its materials and components are reused for a new product.

Greta told the world leaders at Davos to go circular or go home.

Co-creation

kokriːˈeɪʃ(ə)n - noun

The action or process of bringing something into existence, together with someone else

creation of a coalition government

Ideation with consumers, or by consumers while you watch from behind a 1-way mirror.

Our R&D team has run out of ideas, so we're opting to co-create some with some random people we plucked from the street.

Normal People	Innovation People

Consumer Centric

kənˈsu mər ˈsɛn trɪk - adjective

When your business decision-making revolves around (pleasing) your consumer base.

In an age of concern about pleasing shareholders over source of business, 'Consumer Centricity' has become a virtue signal.

Many businesses express consumer centricity by taking every decision to focus groups. This is analogous to asking what your friend wants for their birthday, then giving that, and being disappointed they're not happily surprised.

When the snacking brand team asked consumers if they preferred more or less chocolate, they said 'MORE' and now the business case won't close.

Cradle 2 Cradle

ˈkreɪd(ə)lˈtʊˈkreɪd(ə)l - noun

Moving from one baby's bed (or co) to the next.

The desperate, first-time parents moved the crying baby from cradle to cradle until it finally fell asleep.

Rather than cradle-to-grave focus, this more specific spin on sustainability to use the unprocessed, whole end-of-life product as raw material for a new product.

The exasperated operations manager begged the CC2C professors at the conference to come look at what sustainability means in real life.

Crowd Sourcing

kraʊd ˈsɔr sɪŋ - verb

Address a crowd to ask for money, but not a hold-up nor begging.

"Kind people, please give me your money"

Extract money from a crowd of small donors. Upside: fairly anonymous way of raising small sums of cash. Downside: donors think they're buying a finished product that will go to market.

John posted a flashy rendering of his product on a crowdsourcing platform to lure people into funding the idea.

Data Cleaning

ˈdeɪ tə ˈkli nɪŋ - verb

To remove outliers and obvious errors from data sets.

After noticing the thermometer had broken during the 7th of 10 measurement cycles, the laboratory assistant removed the last four sets

When collecting large data sets from messy sources (like panels of uninterested, paid respondents) the incoming material often includes high percentages of unusable garbage.

Having sent out 20,000 surveys on fragranced contact lenses, the lack of serious response drove Janet nuts. Cleaning the data got her a theoretically correct diagnostic though.

Normal People	Innovation People

Data Mining

'deɪ tə 'maɪ nɪŋ - verb

To dig into a data set in search of something valuable.

We're sitting on 2.7 Tb of customer complaint data. Let's mine that for something to improve our customer satisfaction.

If your data set is large enough, you can find any pattern you want. *After two weeks of mining data for interesting findings, the analyst concluded she should have gone in with a couple of hypotheses to save time and now she deserved a gin tonic.*

Design Thinking

dɪ'zaɪn 'θɪŋ kɪŋ - verb

Think like a designer, especially when solving problems. Simple prototypes, aka Minimal Viable Products, are tested to validate solution principles.

The design team spent some time thinking about a good solution for the client's question.

Design Thinking, aka insight-led ideation, aka user-centric problem solving is a new name for an established, very effective way of working through iterations of solutions and testing simple prototypes to progress to a good & viable idea. It's reinvented once every Marketer's career, and about four times during every Designer's career.

Disillusioned by lack of commercial success, the innovation team switched to design thinking in order to get to same great solution a skilled designer would have created at a quarter of the cost in half the time but without the authority.

Design to Value

dɪ'zaɪn tu 'væl yu - noun

Rethink product design and composition to deliver better value, to the manufacturer.

We are going to remove the expensive ingredients from this product and make the new shape 3% smaller, and hope no one notices while I'm still in this job.

A spin on straightforward cost saving, with the liberty to rethink the structure design or recipe. Works well when the resulting design is openly presented to market as the simpler alternative. Works not so well if introduced as a successor to a more premium previous edition.

Inject air bubbles and call it a mousse.

Normal People	Innovation People

Digital

dɪdʒɪt(ə)l - adjective

Relating to, using, or storing data or information in the form of digital signals.

Digital TV, crisper image quality than its analogue predecessor.

Creating a digital version of whatever was analogue, or without data generation capability before. The prize in sight is using this data for further engagement of the customer, the problem ignored is that some product types are impossible to digitize meaningfully in a non-convoluted way (e.g. food, detergents, toasters).

We sell 45 million packs of toilet paper every year. The QR code has been scanned on at least 34 occasions so we are now feverishly analysing the data this digital experience has generated.

Disruption

dɪsˈrʌpʃən - noun

Disturbance

My movie going experience was severely disrupted by loud munching behind me.

A disturbance of a market, via a radical new product or service solution. Oddly, most FMCG companies seek to disrupt their own categories rather than someone else's, which I have tried and failed to understand.

We are market leader in the pedal-bin category, and our main innovation objective is to disrupt the pedal-bin category.

Exit strategy

ˈɛg zɪt ˈstræt ɪ dʒi - noun

A method of departure, planned ahead of the event triggering departure.

The fire brigade insists every building has a proper exit strategy thought through and implemented via signage.

Founders of companies who have no intent to stay for very long once VC funding or IPO is secured, will design an exit strategy that allows them to depart with some cash as soon as possible.

Stay away from any start-up where the founders have an exit strategy but no revenue model. Better: stay away from any start-up with no revenue model.

Gamification

ˌgeɪ mə fɪˈkeɪ ʃən - noun

To turn an activity into a game.

Lizzy trained her dog to fetch the ball, and thus had gamified an otherwise pointless activity.

A method to turn tedious activities into something enjoyable, which people will then do without needing to be paid. A competitive element usually helps, as well as assigning 'levels' of experience to progress through, and virtual badge to be earned.

"You earned the Elephant Trunk medal for finishing that nose spray in one hay fever season!"

Normal People	Innovation People

Hacks

hæks - noun

Breaking into a system to make it operate differently. Often also refers to shortcuts, usually simplifying a chore of some kind.

He hacked his laundry settings to shorten the cycle by half, by adding 2x more detergent.

A new word for 'short workshop', hinting of a more modern way that doesn't involve too many post-its and more smart people. Previously known as 'pressure cooker'.

"Let's do an idea hack! Yay!"

HBR

Acronym

Short for "Harvard Business Review" a magazine published six times a year by Harvard University, Massachusetts.

Sarah read the latest HBR on the train home.

THE TRUTH. HBR Articles are heralded by corporate innovators & marketers as the absolute zenith of what is right or wrong in the world of innovation. Creative agencies preferred source of buzzwords for new proposals.

Why Co-Creation? Ha! Haven't you read the latest in HBR on incubation?

Helicopter with autopilot

ˈhɛl ɪ ˌkɒp tər wɪθ ˈɔ toʊ ˌpaɪ lət – noun

A helicopter that can fly itself in some situations

The helicopter flew itself.

OMG!! IT'S A FLYING CAR!

Incubator

ɪn kyə ˌbeɪ tər – noun

A device to nurture fragile young organisms through an early stage of life.

The prematurely born baby thrived after a difficult few weeks in the incubator

See: '**Accelerator**'

The hair-splitting debate over the differences between an Accelerator and an Incubator left everyone exhausted, annoyed and none the wiser. The chances of success didn't improve either way.

Insight

ˈɪn ˌsaɪt – noun

A deep understanding, of human behaviour.

"OMG that's SO true" versus *"Yeah, true".*

The term 'insight' lost its magical potency around 2012, when it started to be used for any snippet of data, hypothesis, random fact or rumour.

The team browsed the internet for insight into the life of Generation Z.

Normal People	Innovation People

Internet of Things, IoT

ˈɪn tərˌnɛt ʌv θɪŋ - noun

Devices connected via the internet

Our alarm system is IoT enabled, the camera, movement detector and taser all have their own IP address and are controlled by this app.
IoT's valuable application is in devices traditionally connected by cables, or where 'dumb' can be made 'smart' by hooking up to a central server.

To connect an electrical device to any other electrical device, or app - without too much concern about any need or added value from connecting them - and implemented with cheap, inferior programming skills. Known examples are cat feeders that starve cats, barbecues that don't work outside of wifi-range, and we've had connected fridges since 1997 that still no one has found a purpose for.

Wow, I can now toast my bread to perfectly fit my mood by answering the seven simple questions on my phone's MyToast™ app.

Lean startup

lin ˈstartˌʌp - noun

A method of building a business when you don't know if there is a problem to solve, nor what the solution might then be, nor how the money flows.

Lean start-up was heralded as the best innovation approach for large organisations, because that generation of their innovation teams would rather have worked for a startup than a big corporation.

Just don't, please.

"Because our brand had failed to show any meaningful growth over the past 4 years, they agreed the best way forward was to hire 4 college graduates with no category experience and put them in a separate room with a Ping-Pong table to innovate them out of trouble. Now three and a half years in, we're excited to what will come out!"

Omni-channel brand

ʌmnɪ ˈtʃæn l brænd - noun

Covers all channels.

Lego® is an omni-channel brand, with their market manifestations covering product, gaming, social media, movies, television and theme parks,

Every FMCG brand team wants to break out of their mould, and usually refers to Lego® as the aspiring example.

How do we make our world-leading brand of tinned tuna more omni-channel like Lego®?

Pledge
plɛdʒ - noun

Formal word for promise, often expressed to an anonymous audience rather than someone who will hold you accountable.

He pledged to never drink one drop of alcohol again, after 2025.

A nice way for corporate leadership to rally the troops behind an ambitious goal, without too much concern over practicalities of achieving it. Almost without exception the start of a life of pain for middle management.

Snack food CEO's have recently been out-bidding each other for the greenest 2025 pledges.

Pretotype
priːtətʌɪp - noun

A first or preliminary version of a device or product to test solution principles.

The firm is testing a pretotype of the new can opener, to test whether opening it at the bottom really is as good an idea as they hope.

Also known as Minimal Viable Product (MVP), a simplified design to test for viability. Not to be confused with Prototype (full design made by R&D) or Pilot Run (first trials on final production assets).

As Pretotype, the R&D team gave their test panel cereal cracker, a spoonful of strawberry jam and photo of a smiling woman. The results were disappointing and they dropped their hypothesis.

Pivot
ˈpɪv ət - verb

To spin around an axis.

The ballet dancer skilfully and elegantly pivoted from left to right and back.

To change your mind, and your business plan, because the old idea didn't work or you didn't think it through properly. As long as there is an idiot willing to pay, there is no limit to the number of pivots you can make.

They couldn't figure a way to make money from squeezing juice from a pouch but then went bust before they could pivot for the seventh time.

Normal People	Innovation People

Purpose

ˈpɜr pəs - noun

Aspirational goal towards one strives, often immaterial and related to character or state of being.

Charlotte's purpose in life was to visit every capital on the planet starting with a 'C'. But without a penny to spend on travel, she quickly parked the idea of visiting Canberra, Caracas, Cairo, Columbo and Cape Town... and instead settled on Cardiff as the capital of Wales for now.

Retrofitting onto your brand an ethical, aspirational or simply more palatable reason for existence than 'to make money'. The reality of course being that brands who broadcast their (newfound) purpose loudly tend to overlook how genuine purpose drives all brand & organisational actions and not merely their communications.

The brand team campaigned hard across all their social media channels, on how government should be much more ambitious on the sustainability agenda. But journalists quickly spotted they had been fined twice in a year for excess CO2 emissions, and had paid less than 1% in tax for over a decade.

SaaS

Acronym

The conversion of any product or single-use service into subscription service via the internet.

The photo editing software team created a cloud version of their graphics packages and now charges a pay-per-month fee instead of offering the program for sale as they had for decades before.

For software companies, this has been a great way to keep making money well after the upgrades stopped being worth buying the upgrade for. This has alerted manufacturers of physical goods to consider ways of creating services around their products worth paying a subscription for. Works well for business PR, less so for top line revenue.

Having lost the razorblade home delivery wars, the company pivoted to SaaS (Shaving as a Service) and now sends barbers out to their customers bathrooms.

Sprint

sprɪnt - noun

Run at full speed over a short distance.

I saw Charlie sprinting through traffic towards me

Subset or cluster of activities in an Agile process, as part of a series of iterations

We've been in field since sprint #6, and will continue sprinting until the cows come home.

427

Normal People	Innovation People

Storytelling

ˈstɔr i ˌtɛl ɪŋ - verb

Human history is recorded through storytelling.

Patrick's rendition of the miracle was hampered by his lack of storytelling skill.

The magic that ties loose sand into proud shrines of compelling logic. Contrary to fiction writing, or real life, storytelling is explicitly about creating a narrative that holds truths together into a believe whole.

The data analytics team stopped hiring data scientists and instead recruited former movie script writers to create the boardroom reports.

Strategy

ˈstræt ɪ dʒi

///////////////

Tactics, coherent response to event

Tactics

ˈtæk tɪks

Panic, knee-jerk response to event

TED Talk

tɛd tɔk – noun

TED Conferences (acronym for Technology, Entertainment, Design) is an American media organization that posts 20 minute talks online under the slogan "ideas worth spreading"...

"TED Has some great talks on cartooning and art".

On par with HBR articles, but easier to browse and process by innovators with short attention spans. Used by creative agencies to spice up workshop materials with intriguing thought pieces, which is remarkable as it makes the TED presenter appear much more interesting & intelligent than the agency representative.

"♡ OMG SIMON SINEK OMG ♡" babbled the CMO in her newsletter

Transformation

ˌtræns fərˈmeɪ ʃən - noun

Entering a new state of being.

I met Bob when he was a fit young man, but over time he transformed into Bob The Blob.

A rethink of the business' future, ideally to make it resilient to change and thrive in a future somewhere 5-10 years out. Or at least beyond the expected tenure of the leadership team, and setting an aspiring ambition for their successors. Successful transformation is one of the few innovative journeys that has to start top-down, but the challenge in practice is proper follow-through on long time scales.

Just look at Disney® over the past 60 years; there's your benchmark

Normal People	Innovation People

Use Case

yus keɪs - noun

In software engineering, a use case is a list of actions defining the interactions between a role (actor) and a system to achieve a goal.

She demonstrated how her new finance app worked, with a couple of use cases around counting, lending, laundering and hiding small sums of money.

A somewhat paradoxical proof point for explaining how amazing your *new* idea is, by showing how it's already been done before by someone else.

The board wasn't convinced the idea was radical enough, nor that it would provide an ROI worth the risk. So they asked the team to provide a few use cases to help them decide

White space

waɪt speɪs - noun

Empty space in a document, or squash court.

In the formal departure communication, there was no whitespace left for her to scribble her parting message to the team.

A market gap, mystical opportunity that no one, neither in the business nor a competitor has spotted before. In practice, an area the brand itself hasn't operated in, nor a direct competitor. But given the density of consumer offers in any FMCG category the likelihood of such a unicorn opportunity to exist is dismal.

As market leader in shaving cream foam, the board agreed that shaving cream gels was a real white space worth conquering.

Workout session

ˈwɜːkˌaʊt ˈseʃ ən - noun

A period of intense activity.

The Crossfitter® really looked forward to her 5am workout session in the pouring rain.

A new word for "workshop", hinting to something more active than sitting in a chair all day.

We have six workout sessions scheduled and now working out which ones will be live, and which will be run through Teams.

429

Further salutations

A big THANK YOU to my fellow founders and our incredible teams at Happen & Winkle. You are the reason I get out of bed in the morning. Albeit only if I'm not out of bed already for being with my wife and children first.

Another big THANK YOU to all the client teams who not only challenge us daily with delightful innovation questions, but also laugh with us about the peculiarities this work often brings.

And THANK YOU anonymous reader of this book.
I hope it made you smile, it was a pleasure writing. Get in touch to let me know your thoughts, your messages are very welcome.

Thank you all,

Costas Papaikonomou

Twitter: @grumpyinnovator
Email: costas@grumpyinnovator.com

Printed in Poland
by Amazon Fulfillment
Poland Sp. z o.o., Wrocław

83974999R00242